Essential

English

Grammar

Acknowledgement

This book would not have been possible without the positive motivation of my family members and friends.

Preface

This is an attempt to keep basic grammatical items in a single book. The language has been kept simple and lucid to make the reader understand easily.

As a teacher I have seen my students searching grammatical items in various books as there was no single book which could answer them all the questions. I have tried to fulfill the need of such a book which would introduce the students to all the basic grammar items.

The school students would find this book very useful as it would help them in understanding the various concepts of English usage with suitable examples and explanations. Other readers may get benefit from it as it would prove to be a reference book of grammar for them.

The topics like narration, voice, complex and compound sentences which students consider difficult are dealt in detail in this book. The inclusion of ample examples and formulas would generate students' interest that would help understand the topics easily.

The students and other readers must read the book from beginning to end keeping in mind that while studying about any one topic some other grammatical items are necessary to know. Whenever a term comes that you are not familiar with, first go to the index, find out that term, read about it and then go back to the topic that you were studying in sequence.

I hope this book helps you in understanding English Grammar. The suggestion and comments of readers are always welcome.

Sandeep Kumar Jain

About the Book

This book deals in detail with all major grammatical items of English language with ample number of examples and exercises to make the understanding of the concepts possible.

The concepts and terms are defined in simple lucid language and the emphasis is given on full understanding of the topics included. The book will be very much useful to school and college students as well as the people who would like to use it as a reference book of English Grammar.

Contents

Place of Grammar in a language

Many people find themselves uncomfortable when they hear the word 'grammar' as if it is so difficult that nobody can have mastery over it. But it is not so. Grammar is the system of a language. While learning a language it is not necessary to learn grammar first. When a Language takes birth it is in form of vocal symbols. People make some sounds to express themselves, to convey their needs, their feelings, and their reactions. Later these sounds evolve into words, phrases and sentences. Languages are not fixed or static. They change; they evolve according to the needs of the times. Is it necessary to learn and master grammar of a language first to learn a language? Frankly, the answer is 'no'. A large number of people in this world speak their native languages. They start speaking their language in the childhood even before joining any school. They do not know the word 'grammar' then. Thus grammar is not a stumbling block for a learner of a language. But if one is serious about learning a foreign language, and wants to speak and write more perfectly and efficiently then Grammar can help a lot. It is not like games when you learn the rules of a game first and then start playing it. Languages can be imbibed first and perfected by learning grammar later. But certainly rules, structures and traditions of grammar usage will help you speak a language perfectly. Grammar is like a companion in the way of learning a language perfectly. The vocabulary, idioms, phrases, sayings and nuances of a language equally play great roles in having perfection in it. Grammar of a language follows a system. If anyone starts following this system in a positive mindset, without questioning much and posing questions like 'why?', he/she will understand many things easily .After having some idea about this system of a language which we call grammar one can understand many things himself/herself without having to take help of a teacher or looking in a book.

Take grammar positively like a signpost on a road .It leads you, it guides you. It supports you like a companion in finding your way. It helps you reach your destination. And a day comes when you become so accustomed to that way that you are able to lead and guide others.

Some Essential Definitions

Word – Word is the smallest unit of language which means something. It can be spoken and written.

Subject –a noun, noun phrase or pronoun representing the person or thing that performs the action of the verb, about which something is stated. In the passive sentence the subject is affected by the action of the verb.

Direct object – A noun, noun phrase or pronoun that refers to a person or thing that is affected by the action of the verb.

Indirect object- An indirect object comes before the direct object and tells to whom or for whom the action of the verb is done and who is receiving the direct object.

In the sentence 'He gave Raj an apple.' Raj is indirect object while 'apple' is direct object.

Phrase – a group of words without a finite verb, especially one that forms part of a sentence. 'The white horse' and 'on Sunday evening' are phrases.

Noun phrase – A word or group of words in a sentence that behaves in the same way as a noun: i.e., as a subject, an object, a complement, or as the object of a preposition.

In the sentence 'I talked to the owner of the hotel,' 'owner of the hotel' is a noun phrase. It is working as an object of the verb 'talked'.

Adjective phrase- An adjective phrase is a group of words that acts as an adjective. Example -In the sentence, 'Einstein was a man of great knowledge.', 'of great knowledge' is adjective phrase .It qualifies the noun man just as an Adjective does. It therefore does the work of an adjective and is called an Adjective Phrase.

Clause - A group of words that includes a subject and a verb, and forms a sentence or part of a sentence. For example, In the sentence 'Make hay while the sun shines', 'Make hay' is the main clause and 'while the sun shines' is the subordinate clause.

Sentence - A set of words expressing a statement, a question or an order, usually containing a subject and a verb.

Particle -an adverb or a preposition that can combine with a verb to make a phrasal verb. In 'He gave up that job'; the word 'up' is a particle.

Finite verb- A finite verb form shows a particular tense, person and number. 'Am', 'is', 'are', 'was' and 'were' are the finite forms of 'be'.

Non finite verb- a non-finite verb form does not show a particular tense, person or number. 'Being' and 'been' are the non-finite forms of verb 'be'.

Genitive - a special form of a noun, a pronoun or an adjective that is used to show possession or close connection between two things. Ex: Ram's copy, his belief, son of Mr. Pal, girl's poem etc.

1. Articles

Let us begin with a story.

Once there lived **a** hen near **the** sea shore. She used to watch **the** sea creatures all **the** day. One night she saw **a** dream. In **the** dream she saw that **an** octopus came out of **the** sea and started living on **the** sea shore with **the** hen. **The** hen took care of him. She arranged for food for **the** octopus. **The** octopus tasted **an** apple one day. He liked **the** apple very much. **The** hen began to collect apples for him. She invited other creatures to introduce Octopus to them. She took consent of every creature that they would not harm **the** octopus in any way. Very soon **the** octopus became habitual of living on **the** sea shore. It was **a** unique kind of friendship in which **a** creature of **the** sea was living with surface animals. Gradually **the** octopus began to appreciate the feel of rain and snowfall on his body. He could see flowers, rainbow and greenery with open eyes. He could touch **the** objects with his hands. He could enjoy **the** evening breeze. **The** stars appeared at night to greet him. They were surprised that a strange animal was living on **the** surface which they had never seen before. How could **the** stars see such **an** animal which lived always under water! But soon **the** octopus began to miss his original home. He was now always thinking about **the** sea grass. He wanted to float in water again and move with little efforts in limitless expanse of water. He wanted to see **the** other creatures of **the** sea. He was upset. **The** hen saw his depressed face one day and knew immediately that he was no longer interested in living on **the** Earth's surface. So she collected all **the** creatures and arranged **a** farewell party. The octopus said thanks to them and moved to **the** sea which welcomed him with love.

Now read the story again and find the word 'a', 'an' and 'the' in it. Try to understand the reason of their use.

Now look at these words:

A ball   **a cap**   **an elephant**   **an orange**

an igloo   **an eye**   **a song**   **the Sea**

the moon   **the President**   **the Andes**   **the Pacific Ocean**

We can see the difference. Why some of these begin with 'a', some with 'an' and some with 'the'? It is because of a tradition of using different article before different kind of words. This tradition follows a pattern which we need to know.

Before beginning it must be noted that

Apple, bag, chair, day etc. – such things which we can count are called countable.

Milk, water, air, salt, sugar etc. _ such things which we cannot count are called uncountable.(these things can be measured and felt but cannot be counted.)

When we say about one thing /person we refer to it as singular.

When we say about more than one thing/ person we refer to them as plural.

In grammar, a type of determiner that precedes a noun is called article.

Basically there are two types of articles in English: the definite article (the) and the indefinite article (a/an).

Definite article 'the'- 'The' is used with definite things/posts/great rivers/great mountains/great books etc.

Indefinite article 'a/an'- 'An' is used before singular countable nouns beginning with vowel sound.

'A' is used before singular countable noun beginning with consonant sound.

A and an with singular nouns

1. We use **'a'** with singular nouns which begin with consonant sounds.
Example-a book, a man a horse, a uniform (sounds like 'yu-niform')

a book	a cat	a dog	a fan
a gun	a hen	a jug	a kite
a lion	a mango	a nest	a parrot
a queen	a rabbit	a son	a toy
a van	a wire	a xylophone	a yellow box
a zebra	a European	a useful book	a one-eyed person

2. We use **'an'** with singular nouns which begin with vowel sounds.
Example- an airplane   an hour (sounds like –'our')

	an x-ray (sounds like 'ex-ray')		
an exercise			
an owl	an orange	an eagle	an inkpot
an ape	an arrow	an ear	an image
an enquiry	an uncle	an ugly crone	an armed soldier
an hour	an heir	an octopus	an honest boy
an orphan	an ox	an aunt	an urban house

3. We use indefinite article **'a/an'** when we speak of someone or something for the first time.

Example-We saw an artist painting by the river.
A stranger knocked at our door.

Practice   A

Fill in the blanks with 'a' or 'an'.

1…….airport	2……baton	3…..elephant
4…..flower	5…….hourglass	6…..iron
7…….racquet	8…….seed	9…..umpire
10….woman	11……hour	12…..table

Practice B

Fill in the blanks with a/an.
1. That is ……UFO.
2………………ostrich is…………bird.
3. Joseph wants to be …………engineer.
4. This is not …….ape. It is ……gorilla.
5. There is …….pond in Mary's garden.
6. John bought ………..atlas and………….dictionary.

Practice C

Complete the table-

	a	**an**
1.animal	c-w	a-t
2.bird	-r-w	-a-le
3.building	-ch-ol	-ff-ce
4.flower	-os-	-rch-d
5.food	- a-d-w-ch	-c- cr-am
6.object	-a-nco-t	-mbr-ll-

Practice D

Use 'a' or 'an' before these nouns-
1. Mr Roy is………..journalist.
2. Shikha is ………..officer.
3. Dhirendra is ……singer.
4. Mohanti is………teacher.

5. Roshan is …Police officer.
6. Narendra is ………..lawyer.
7. John was ………..… engineer.

Practice E

Fill in the blanks choosing the right option.
1. Dinesh drew an ....and a ....in his sketch book. [adult/child]
2. We saw an ....and a...........on the stage. [Elephant/giraffe]
3. This pendant has both an ....and a ....in it. [diamond/ emerald]
4. I use a ....to add numbers. Some people prefer to use an ....
[Abacus/calculator]

Article 'the'

[1] We use article 'the' when a person, an animal, a plant, a place or a thing is mentioned a second time.

Examples :

I bought a book this morning .I am now reading the book.
There is a spot on your collar. You can use lime and salt to remove the spot.
[2] We use article 'the' when it is clear to the listener or reader which person, animal, plant, place or thing we are referring to.
Example-: The judge found him not guilty.(= the judge in charge of his trial)
    I need to go to the bathroom.(= the bathroom in this building)
[3] We use 'the' when there is only one such thing.
  Example- The Earth goes round the sun.
          Dina's dream is to sail around the world.
[4] We usually use 'the' before ordinal numbers.-
Examples- I live on the third floor.
          My birth day is on the second of June.
[5] 'the' is used before superlative degree of adjective-
The best boy, the highest peak, the greatest musician, the longest tunnel
[6] The is used before name of famous building and public place-
The India Gate, The Red Fort, The White house, The Great Wall of China
[7] We use 'the' before some proper nouns such as-

A) The names of oceans, rivers, seas and straits

The Pacific Ocean   The Nile (river)   The Red Sea

[8] We use 'the' before the names of most buildings, landmarks and natural wonders-

Example- The Grand hotel   The Taj Mahal   The Gate way of India

[9]. The names of places containing of
        The Republic of China
        The University of Manchester
[10] The names of places ending in plural
        The British Isles   The Netherlands

[11] 'the' is used before names of newspaper and magazines.
The times of India, The Washington Post , The India Today ,The Time.
[12] We use 'the' before the names of political parties, Nation and Religious group.
The French, the Indian National Congress, the Hindu
[13] Use of 'the' before the names of historical events
The Quit India movement, The French Revolution, The Renaissance

[14] 'the' is used before parts of day
In the evening, in the afternoon, in the morning
[15] 'the' is used before names of mountain ranges ,rivers, islands, deserts etc.
        The Amazon   The Himalaya
        The Caspian lake   The Andaman Nicobar islands
        The Sahara Desert   The Andes
[16] When an adjective us used as a noun then article 'the' is used.
        The poor   the needy   the rich
[17] In sentences of comparison 'the' is used twice. The comparative degree is used in both places.
Example:
The more you practice the more you become perfect.

The more you run the more you lose weight.

The harder he worked the more he was criticized.

Practice F

Fill in the blanks with 'a', 'an' or 'the'.

1. There is …………owl on my roof. My cat is watching ………..owl with great interest.

2. There are dark clouds in ………..sky. We can't see ……..sun.

3. Don't stand at ………..door, Marina. You are blocking ………..way.

4. I gave my brother …………xylophone for his birthday .Now he plays …………xylophone every day.

5. Mr.Gupta is looking for …………architect to design his house. ………..architect must be good.

Practice G

Fill in the blanks with 'a', 'an' or 'the'.

There is (1) ----------shopping mall on Hicks street with five fast food outlets, two department stores, (2) ---------- amusement centre and (3) ---- musical fountain. All (4) ---------- shop units are occupied, but there is (5) ----------- unit on (6) ---------- ground floor next to (7) ---------- musical fountain that is empty. This unit can be rented for Rs.8000 (8) ---------- month. So far, only (9) ---------- ice –cream café has shown interest in renting (10) ----------unit.

Practice H

Rewrite the sentences. Put 'a', 'an' or 'the' in the correct places.

1. Sea is calm today.

   …………………..

2. Would you like ice cube in your drink?

   …………………….

3. Lisa uses apron when she cooks.

   ………………………………..

4. I have orange and pear. I'll keep orange. Who wants pear?

   ………………………………..

5. My father works in bank. He leaves house at 8.00 a.m. and arrives at office at 8.30 am.

   ………………………………..

Practice I

Fill suitable article in the blanks.

1. I have a guitar. My brother bought ………..guitar in Spain.
2. I live in Surat. My house is near ……………Sea.
3. I will attend a conference in Australia next month. ------------- Conference will be at ------------University of New South Wales.
4……………National Museum is on ---------Gandhi Road. It is next to …………Taj Hotel.

Uses of Articles

<u>With countable and uncountable nouns</u>

Countable nouns-
      Cake, drum, leaf, bat, table, ball
Uncountable nouns-
      Bread, sand, rain, soil, milk, air, time

1. We use 'a' or 'an' with uncountable nouns in this way-
    a/an +countable noun + of + uncountable noun
  Example- Seema drinks a cup of tea every morning.
        Manish bought a loaf of bread.
        Hari drank a glass of milk.
        Seema took a piece of cloth.
        They need a bag of rice.

2. We use 'the' with uncountable nouns when it is clear to the listener or reader which things we are referring to. We do not use 'the' with uncountable nouns when we are talking in general.
        Example-The rice in this supermarket is cheap.
            Rice is the main food of South Indians.

Practice J

Fill in the blanks with a, an, the

1. We need air to live, but ………..air in our cities is polluted.

2. Mr.Sharma had …….plate of fried noodles for lunch. Mrs.Sharma had …….bowl of soup.

3………..money in that box is mine, and ………money on that table is yours.

4. Look! There is snow on …..ground. ………snow makes the place look beautiful.

5. We own ….. acre of land outside Mumbai.

Pronunciation of 'the'

Da (if following word begins with consonant)(See Oxford Advanced Leaners Dictionary)	Di (if following word begins with vowel) (See Oxford Advanced Leaners Dictionary)
The girl	The English girl
The book	The orange book
The school	The old school
The unit (here pronunciation of 'u' is like a consonant-yu)	The uncle (here pronunciation of ' u' is like a vowel)

Illustrations-

There is no need of any definite article with general indefinite words	Definite article should be used with definite words
Life is too short. I like flowers.	I've read a book on the life of Bill Clinton. I like the flowers in your garden.
There is no need of any definite article with the names of persons in singular ,relatives	Definite article is used with nationality, family Names in plural
Kailash, Rohan,Mary	The Smiths live in Chicago. The Indians are honest people.

There is no need of definite article with public buildings ,institutions ,means of transport (indefinite).	Definite article is used with public buildings, institutions and means of transport (definite).
Mohan doesn't like to go to school. We go to school by bus. Some people go to church on Sundays.	The bus to Agra leaves at 10.50. The school Mohan goes is old. The round church at Goa is famous.
There is no need of definite article with the name of countries in singular ,summit of mountains ,continents, towns	Definite article is used with name of countries in plural, Mountain ranges and Regions.
France, Mt.Everest, Africa ,New York ,New Delhi	The U.S.A , The Alps, The West of Australia
There is no need of definite article with the name of single island.	definite article is used with the name of group of islands
Sicily	The Bahamas ,The British Isles ,The Andaman and Nicobar islands
There is no need of definite article with the names of parks ,streets , lakes etc.	Definite article is used with of - phrase, oceans ,seas ,rivers
Central Park , Mount Road ,Oxford Street	The Statue of liberty, The Atlantic ocean, The Suez canal, The Ganges
There is no need of definite article with names of months ,days of the week(indefinite)	definite article is used with the names of months ,days of the week(definite)
The weekend is over on Monday morning. The vacation starts in May.	I always remember the Monday when I had an accident. He was married in the June of 2007.

Omission of articles-

In the following cases articles are omitted.

1. Names of languages and nationalities – Chinese, English, Russian, and Spanish (unless we are referring to the population of the nation.

   Example- The Spanish are known for their hospitality.

2. Names of sports –Volleyball, Cricket ,Football ,Tennis

3. Names of academic subjects- mathematics, History, Geography, Chemistry.

Practice K

Fill in the blanks with suitable article –
1. I like ……..blue T-shirt over there better than ………..red one.
2. That car does 150 miles …………hour.
3. Where is ………… diary I lent you yesterday.
4. Do you still live in ………Bhopal.
5. Is your father working in …………old office building.
6. Amar's father works as ………..electrician.
7. The Tomatoes are 15Rs ……..kilo.
8. Basu has …………. terrible head ache.
9. After this tour you have ………..whole afternoon free to explore …………city.

Answers of practice exercises
Practice A. 1.an 2.a 3.an 4.a 5.an 6.an 7.a 8.a 9.an 10.a 11.an 12.a
Practice B. 1. a 2.an,a 3.an 4.an,a 5a . 6. an, a
Practice C. 1.cow, ant 2.crow,eagle 3.school,office 4.rose,orchid 5.sandwich ,ice-cream 6.raincoat, umbrella
Practice D. 1. a 2.an 3.a 4.a 5.a 6.a 7an
Practice E. 1. adult ,child, 2.elephant,giraffe 3.emerald ,diamond 4.calculator,abacus
Practice F. 1. an, the 2.the,the 3.the,the 4.a,the 5.an,the
Practice G. 1.a 2.an 3.a 4.the 5.a 6.the 7.the 8.a 9.an 10.the
Practice H. 1. The Sea is calm today.
2. Would you like an ice cube in your drink?
3. Usha uses an apron when she cooks.
4. I have an orange and a pear. I'll keep the orange. Who wants the pear?
5. My father works in a bank. He leaves house at 8.00 a.m. and arrives at the office at 8.30 a.m.

Practice I. 1. the 2.the 3.the ,the 4.the,the,the
Practice J. 1. the 2.a,a 3.the,the 4.the,the 5.an
Practice K. 1.the, the 2.an 3.the 4.no article 5.an 6.an 7.a 8.a, the 9.the, the

2. **Parts of Speech**

Words function in eight different ways in sentences. According to their functions they have been divided in eight different groups .These groups are called parts of speech. The parts of speech are named thus-

1. Noun
2. Pronoun
3. Adjective
4. Verb
5. Adverb
6. Preposition
7. Conjunction
8. Interjection

2.1 Noun

Let us begin with a story:

One day some **creatures** like **Hyper hen**, **Rapid rabbit** and **Speedy squirrel** insisted that they would sit on the back of the **Ortho octopus** and travel on it. They went to the **ostrich's home** and expressed their desire to travel on his back. But the **ostrich** thought that it will be against his dignity that he would carry some lesser **birds** on his back. So he refused to do so. Now the hen, rabbit and squirrel came back .They were sad but they decided that they would anyhow fulfill their desire keeping in mind that the self respect of ostrich must not be hurt.

The idea came in the hen's mind that if the three small creatures do some favour to the octopus, the later would be agree to take them on his back to return the favour. The three then decided to meet at a shore on **the Indian Ocean** and to wait for some suitable opportunity to help **the octopus**. Then the expected day arrived suddenly. One day some **fishermen** have spread their net to catch **fish** in the ocean. The shoal of fish was busy in laying eggs in the hidden spot of **the sea** that day so no fish was caught in the net. But unfortunately the octopus came in that direction and was badly caught in **the net**. His **limbs** were so badly entangled in the net that he could not free himself. The three friends saw octopus caught in the net and decided to help him. When the **fisherman** brought the net back he was upset to find that he did not get any fish that day. But he was not completely at loss because at least a big octopus was there to feed on. He kept the net on a boat and began to wait for other fishermen. **The rabbit** got an opportunity to jump on **that boat** on which the octopus was lying helplessly. He cut the net immediately and set octopus free. The squirrel gave him some **nuts** to eat and the hen sprinkled some **water** on him to make him feel comfortable. The octopus was very much thankful to all of them. He expressed his **thankfulness** again and again and insisted on doing something for them to return the **favour**. But the three did not ask for anything. In a few days the octopus got completely well and came to the **seashore** to meet the three friends. He remembered the desire of the three to travel on his back. He immediately called them for a **ride**. The three agreed this time as octopus was willingly calling them. Thus the **desire** of the three was fulfilled.

Definition –Noun is the name of a person, place, thing, quality, collection, material, state, attitude etc.

Ram	Geeta	Bhopal	The Ganga
The Yamuna	bag	beauty	team
Milk	school	river	bottle

Person	Ram, Geeta
Place	School, river
Thing	bottle, coat,
Quality	sincerity
Collection	bunch ,class, army, herd
Material	milk ,water, salt, sugar, petrol
State	sleep, hunger, thirst, happiness, worry, anxiety , prosperity, poverty gladness, alertness ,curiosity
Attitude	Willingness, ignorance, readiness, negligence, preference ,sincerity, honesty

Types and Forms of noun-

1. **Proper noun-** a noun that names a particular person, place or thing and always begins with a capital letter.

   Ex. Ram, The Ganga, Africa and New Year, Gwalior, Sunday , June

   If a proper noun has two or more words each word is written in capital letter-

   Mahatma Gandhi, London Bridge, the Indian Ocean, the Bay of Bengal,

2. **Common noun-**A common noun is a name given to every person, thing or place of the same class or kind. For example dog and paper are common nouns but Mary and New York are proper nouns
   Ex. Boy, Girl, City, Country, Book, river, town, mountain, lake, leader

3. **Collective noun** - a noun that refers to a group of people, animals or objects, for example; team or family. In British English it can be followed by either a singular verb or a plural verb. In American English it is always followed by a singular verb.

   Ex. Flock, crowd, army, fleet, family, nation, parliament, committee, bunch, pack, herd

4. **Concrete nouns-** a noun that refers to an object that you can see or touch, not to an idea or feeling.

   Ex. table, chair, stone, milk, wall, window, door

5. **Gerund or Verbal Noun**- a noun formed by adding -ing to a verb, that describes an action, such as running or believing.

   Ex. - singing, dancing, reading, playing, and sleeping.
   Writing is my hobby.
   Gardening is his favourite pastime.
   Reading is a good habit.

6. **Nominative** - The form of the noun or pronoun when it is the subject of a verb.
   Ex.   Ram plays cricket.
         The Sun rises in the east.

   7. **Direct object**- The noun or pronoun that is affected by the action of a transitive verb .In the sentence 'Hari was reading a book. The noun phrase 'a book' is the direct object of the verb was reading.

   8. **Indirect object**-The person or thing in a sentence that is indirectly affected by the action of the verb because something is given to them or done to them.

   Ex. 'He gave Ram a book.'

Here 'Ram' is the indirect object of the verb give.

   9. **Abstract noun**-a noun that refers to a quality, idea, feeling, action or state.

   Ex. Brevity is the soul of wit.
      Wisdom is better than strength.
      Health is wealth.
Some of the abstract nouns are -Beauty, Ugliness, dearness, length, height, weight, honesty, poverty, clarity, purity, pity, anger

These nouns can be divided into various groups-

Quality- Hardness, Softness, wisdom, honesty, bravery, cowardice, treachery, purity, ability, partiality, courage

<u>Action</u>-Activity, race, judgment, theft, decision, revision, speech, exercise, practice

<u>State</u>-Illness, happiness, sadness, boyhood, childhood, death, birth, teenage, adulthood, poverty, opulence.

10. Uncountable noun- a noun that does not have a plural form and cannot be counted.

Ex. Furniture, milk, water, sand, oil, time, oxygen, air, ink, bread, salt, sugar, diesel, Petrol

11. Genitive-a form of the noun or pronoun used to show possession .In English this is shown by adding 's' at the end of the word. For example - <u>Satish's</u> birthday.

Ex. - Car's window, Cow's tail

Some examples of collective noun-

These collective nouns are commonly used under the category of people.

1. A class of students.
2. An army of soldiers.
3. A choir of singers.
4. A crew of sailors.
5. A band of musicians.
6. A bunch of crooks.
7. A gang of thieves.
8. A group of dancers.
9. A team of players.
10. A pack of thieves.
11. A troupe of artists/dancers.
12. A staff of employees.
13. A regiment of soldiers.
14. A tribe of natives.
15. An audience of listeners.
16. A panel of experts.
17. A gang of labourers.
18. A flock of tourists.
19. A board of directors.
20. A crowd of people/spectators

The following collective nouns are used for animals.

1. A catch of fish.
2. An army of ants.
3. A flight of birds.
4. A flock of birds.
5. A haul of fish.
6. A flock of sheep.

7. A hive of bees.
8. A litter of cubs.
9. A host of sparrows.
10. A team of horses.
11. A troop of lions.
12. A zoo of wild animals.
13. A pack of wolves.
14. A litter of puppies/kittens.
15. A murder of crows.
16. A kennel of dogs.

17. A pack of hounds/dogs.
18. A swarm of bees/ants/rats/flies.
19. A team of horses/ducks/oxen
20. Shoal of fish
21. A herd of deer/ cattle/ elephants/ goats /buffaloes.

The following collective nouns are used for things.

1. A group of islands.
2. A galaxy of stars.
3. A wad of notes.
4. A forest of trees.
5. A stack of wood.
6. A fleet of ships.
7. A string of pearls.
8. A hedge of bushes.
9. A library of books.
10. A basket of fruit.
11. A bowl of rice.
12. A pack of cards.

13. A pair of shoes.
14. A bouquet of flowers.
15. A bunch of keys.
16. A chest of drawers.
17. A pack of lies.
18. A range of mountains.
19. A cloud of dust.
20. An album of stamps / autographs/photographs.

Practice 2A

Choose the correct option-

1. A shoal of…………..	a. fish	b. birds
2. A ……playing cards.	a. flock	b. pack
3. A choir of ………….	a. artists	b. singers
4. A ………...of events.	a. series	b. bunch
5. A……….....…of keys.	a. group	b. bunch
6. A pack of ……………	a. dogs	b. cats
7. A herd of ……………	a. lions	b. cattle
8. A swarm of …………	a. bees	b. bears

Answers: 1.fish 2.pack 3.singers 4. Series5. bunch 6. dogs 7.cattle 8.bees.

Practice 2B

Choose the correct option-

1. A flock of	a. lions	b. birds
2. A chest of	a. drawers	b. cupboards
3. A fleet of	a. airplanes	b. ships
4. A range of	a. flowers	b. mountains
5. A bouquet of	a. keys	b. flowers
6. A galaxy of	a. bushes	b. stars

Answers:1. Birds 2. Drawers3. Ships 4.mountains 5.flowers 6.stars.

Practice 2C

Fill in the blanks with the correct forms of the given nouns for the following exercise. Use each noun only once.

Chair	job	hair	works	luggage
experience	Furniture	information	progress	permission

1. I don't have much..................just two small bags.
2. They are going to tell you all you want to know. They are going to give you a lot of................
3. There is room for everybody to sit down. There are a lot of   ....
4.We have no.............., not even a bed or a table.
5. 'What does Alok look like?' 'He's got a long beard and very short............
6. Kavita's English is very bad. She must make...................... .
7. Neeraj is unemployed. He's looking for a ....
8. If you want to leave work early, you have to ask for ....
9. I don't think Amita will get the job. She hasn't got enough ....
10.Ravindra Nath Tagore's .... are wonderful.

Answers-1.luggage 2.information 3.chairs 4.furniture 5.hair 6.progress
7.job 8.permission 9.experience 10.works

Practice 2D

1. Match the nouns with their forms-

Noun	Form
a. Boy, Girl, City	1. Genitive
b. Mohan, Deepak, Reshu	2. Common Noun
c. Singing, dancing ,painting	3. Proper Noun
d. Rahul's ,Dinesh's, Arvind's	4. Material Noun
e. Sugar ,Salt, Oil	5. Abstract noun
f. Happiness, Beauty, Tiredness	6. Count Noun
g. day, chair, book	7. Objective Case
h. bunch, herd, flock, crowd	8. Subjective Case
i. <u>Mohan</u> works hard.	9. Gerund
j. They call <u>Mohan.</u>	10.Collective Noun .

Answers: a -2, b-3, c-9, d-1 , e-4 ,f-5, g- 6 ,h-10 ,i-8, j-7

Noun: Numbers

1. Singular number –A noun that points out one person or thing is called to be in the singular number.

Example: Cat, dog, bird, cow, boy, girl, man, woman, star, tree, pen, pencil, ship

2. Plural number-A noun that points out more than one person or thing is said to be in the plural number.

Ex.-cats, dogs, birds, cows, boys, girls, men, women, stars, trees ,pens, pencils, ships, etc.

Singular	Plural	Singular	Plural
sheep	sheep	boy	boys
copy	copies	girl	girls
trolly	trollies	man	men
hand	hands	woman	women
paper	papers	toy	toys
bag	bags	ox	oxen
pencil	pencils	fish	fish

Changing from singular noun to plural noun-

Rule 1.in most of the nouns we can make plural by adding –s in it.

No.	Singular	Plural	No.	Singular	Plural
1	boy	boys	11	crow	crows
2	girl	girls	12	daughter	daughters
3	bee	bees	13	farmer	farmers
4	cock	cocks	14	girl	girls
5	cat	cats	15	hat	hats
6	dog	dogs	16	master	masters
7	doll	dolls	17	star	stars
8	ear	ears	18	Teacher	teachers
9	hen	hens	19	window	windows
10	jaw	jaws	20	year	years

Rule2 .Nouns ending in 'ss', 'sh', 'ch', or 'x' can be changed into plural by adding 'es' in them.

No.	singular	Plural	No.	singular	Plural
1	ass	asses	9	house	houses
2	class	classes	10	kiss	kisses
3	bench	benches	11	loss	losses
4	box	boxes	12	Match	Matches
5	dish	dishes	13	pass	passes
6	fox	foxes	14	patch	patches
7	gas	gases	15	quiz	quizzes
8	glass	glasses	16	tax	taxes

Exceptions to rule2

	Singular	plural
1	analysis	analyses
2	monarch	monarchs
3	stomach	stomachs
4	locus	loci
5	radius	radii
6	ox	oxen

Rule 3. If any noun ending with 'O' has any consonant before it then 'es' is added in it to make it plural.

	singular	plural
1.	buffalo	buffaloes
2	cargo	cargoes
3	echo	echoes
4	hero	heroes
5	mango	mangoes
6	motto	mottoes
7	mosquito	mosquitoes
8	negro	negroes
9	potato	potatoes
10	tomato	tomatoes
11	volcano	volcanoes

Exceptions to rule 3-

Canto   Cantos
Dynamo   Dynamos
Photo   Photos
Zero   Zeros

Rule 4. If any noun ends with double vowel, 's' is added into it to make it a plural.

No.	Singular	Plural
1.	Bamboo	Bamboos
2.	Bee	Bees
3	Cuckoo	Cuckoos
4	Portfolio	Portfolios
5	Radio	Radios
6	Studio	Studios
7	Tree	Trees
8	Woe	Woes
9	Zoo	Zoos

Rule 5. If a noun ends with –y ,and consonant comes before –y, then 'y' is removed and –ies is added to make it's plural.

1.	army	armies	9	Diary	diary
2	baby	babies	10	Duty	duties
3	belly	bellies	11	fairy	fairies
4	body	bodies	12	family	families
5	city	cities	13	luxury	luxuries
6	copy	copies	14	pony	ponies
7	country	countries	15	story	stories
8	cry	cries	16	victory	victories

Rule 6. If noun ends in'-y and a vowel comes before '–y', then 's' is added to make it's plural.

1.	boy	boys	7.	play	plays
2.	day	days	8.	valley	valleys
3.	donkey	donkeys	9.	chimney	chimneys
4.	joy	joys	10.	Ray	rays
5.	essay	essays	11.	toy	toys
6.	key	keys	12.	way	ways

Rule7. If noun ends in 'f', or 'fe, then 'fe' is removed and ' –ves' is added to make its plural-

1.	calf	calves	7.	leaf	leaves
2.	half	halves	8.	thief	thieves
3.	elf	elves	9.	scarf	scarves
4.	knife	knives	10.	shelf	shelves
5.	wife	wives	11.	wife	wives
6.	loaf	loaves	12.	wolf	wolves

Exception to Rule 7

1	belief	beliefs	6	safe	safes
2	chief	chiefs	7	grief	griefs
3	cliff	cliffs	8	mischief	mischiefs
4	dwarf	dwarfs	9	handkerchief	handkerchiefs
5	roof	roofs	10	staff	staffs

Rule8. In some nouns some letters are changed to make plurals-

1.	Foot	Feet
2	Goose	Geese
3	Louse	Lice
4	Man	Men
5	Mouse	Mice
6	Tooth	Teeth
7	Woman	Women
8	Washer man	Washer men
9.	Brother	Brethren
10.	child	children
11.	Ox	Oxen

Rule9.Some nouns are made plural by adding-'en' to them.

1	brother	brothern
2	child	children
3	ox	oxen

Rule 10. If ex, is, on, um, us or a comes in the end of a noun then –ices, -es, -a, i, ae respectively is added to change them into plurals-

1.	Index	Indices
2..	Vertex	Vertices
3.	Axis	Axes
4.	Criterion	Criteria
5.	Curriculum	Curricula
6.	Medium	Media
7.	Focus	Foci
8.	Locus	Loci
9.	formula	formulae

Exercise- Complete the exercise with correct forms of the given nouns. Use each noun only once.

man	box	match	tooth
discovery	ox	piano	beach
cliff	laboratory	Medium	attorney

1. The age at which the first tooth appears differs greatly from child to child. Very occasionally, children are born with one or more.............

2. I need some ....to light the fire.

3. Studies are showing that..................process information differently from women.

4. Meena needed some legal advice for her businesses, so she contacted two................... .

5. New scientific ....are made every day in ......throughout the world.

6. The farmer loaded his cart with ....of fresh vegetables to take to market .His cart was pulled by two................ .

7. The north side of the island has no.................for people to walk on. There are only steep ....No one climb these steep walls of rock.

8. The music building at the university has 26 ....for students to play on.

9. People get most of their news about the world through the mass...... that is, through radio, television, the internet, newspapers, and magazines.

Answers: 1.teeth 2. Matches 3.Men 4. Attorneys 5.discoverioes, laboratories 6.boxes, oxen 7.beech, cliffs 8.pianos 9.media

Noun: Gender

English nouns can be categorized in four kinds of genders.

1. Masculine Gender- A noun is said to be in the Masculine gender if it refers to a male character or member of a species.

Man, tiger, hero, boy, king, horse, nephew, and actor

2. **Feminine Gender-** A noun is said to be in feminine gender if it refers to a female member of a species.

Woman, tigress, heroine, girl, mare, niece, empress, and actress are few of the feminine gender.

3. Common Gender-a noun is said to be in common gender if it refers to a member of species which can be male or female.

Child, student, friend, player, candidate, servant, client

4. Neuter Gender-A noun is said to be in neuter gender if it refers to a member of a species which is neither a male nor a female. Normally lifeless objects are kept in this category.

Chair, table, tree, paper, mountain, street, book, car, computer are some of the nouns of neuter gender.

Some examples of masculine and feminine genders are as given below-

Masculine	Feminine	Masculine	Feminine
boy	girl	actor	actress
man	woman	poet	poetess
cow	bull	cock	hen
hero	heroine	peacock	peahen
shepherd	shepherdess	horse	mare
duke	duchess	gentleman	lady
waiter	waitress	son	daughter

Rules of changing from Masculine to Feminine gender are as given below-

Rule1: We add –ess in masculine gender to make it feminine.

Masculine	Feminine	Masculine	Feminine
Author	Authoress	Tailor	Tailoress
Baron	Baroness	Tutor	Tutoress
Count	Countess	Steward	Stewardess
Giant	Giantess	Shepherd	Shepherdess
Lion	Lioness	Mayor	Mayoress
Host	Hostess	Poet	Poetess

Rule 2: By removing last vowel and adding –ess in the end.

Masculine	Feminine	Masculine	Feminine
actor	actress	prince	princess
director	directress	tiger	tigress
editor	editress	waiter	waitress
hunter	huntress	traitor	traitress
monitor	monitress	elector	electress
negro	negress	porter	portress

Rule 3: by adding a word in the beginning or end of a noun

Milk man	Milk maid
Man servant	maid servant
Doctor	lady doctor
Peacock	peahen
Land lord	landlady
Father in law	mother in law
Brother in law	sister in law
Step father	step father
He goat	she goat
Bull calf	cow calf
Tom cat	she cat
Step brother	step sister
Head master	head mistress

Grandson   grand daughter
Great uncle   great aunt

Rule4: Some other masculine nouns are changed into feminine by adding –ess in the end and changing the original word a little.

duke	duchess
emperor	empress
god	goddess
governor	governess
master	mistress
marquis	marquise
sorcerer	sorceress

Rule5: Some masculine nouns are changed into feminine by using entirely different word.

Masculine	Feminine	Masculine	Feminine
Buck	Doe	Earl	Countess
Boar	Sow	Father	Mother
Cock	Hen	Boy	Girl
Drake	Duck	Sire	Dame
Dog	Bitch	Sir	Madam
Drone	Bee	Uncle	Aunt
Bull	Cow	Boy	Girl
gander	goose	Gentleman	Lady
horse	Mare	Man	Woman
Ram	Ewe	Nephew	Niece
Fox	Vixen	Husband	Wife
Wizard	Witch	bridegroom	Bride

2.2 Pronoun

Let us read a story to better understand the use of pronoun.

There was a pond at the edge of the village Rampur. A buffalo and a crane were always seen there in the company of each other. The crane used to sit on buffalo's back and ate the flea that troubled **her.** In this way **he** got all the food that **he** needed. Their companionship was going on for more than two years. **They** were happy in the company of each other. But one day something unfortunate happened.

The buffalo's tail was getting heavy with the mud of the side of the pond. **She** waved it with great effort so that the mud may be thrown away and it may become light. By accident the tail hit the crane who could not imagine that it would suddenly come towards him. **He** blamed buffalo for **her** rude behavior. The buffalo did not consider **herself** guilty .**She** thought it was natural on **her** part to wave her tail. "**I** made no mistake consciously" she said. **She** too blamed the crane for being careless and ignorant, "Couldn't **you** take care of **yourself**?" Thus the two close friends stopped talking to each other. This went on for a few days .But soon the buffalo felt the need of the crane as the flea on her body started pestering **her**. **She** used to rub **her** sides with a wooden pole and got some relief but **she** could not rub all parts of **her** body. She felt an itching all over **her** body and wanted immediate relief. **She** was feeling helpless. **She** remembered the days when crane used to sit on **her** back and removed the flea from the entangled hair thus giving her relief form etching. She felt that **she** has lost a friend who used to give her relief. Now who would talk to **her**? She considered **herself** lonely and helpless. Whom can **she** call to remove the flea from **her** body? Which bird or animal could take place of the crane?

The crane too was upset. **He** got few worms to eat .None of the other birds help him. Not only had **he** lost a source of food but also a companion who spent whole day with him. Both of **them** felt the need of one another. Each of them felt that they should revive their friendship. Either of the two might take the initiative. Then one day the crane saw that buffalo's tail was covered with mud badly and she is feeling difficulty in moving it. This sight touched him deeply. He realized that the buffalo was not wrong on **her** part when she moved her tail as it was heavy and difficult to move. He blamed **himself** for bringing the friendship to an end. **He** thought that he should take the initiative himself so he went to the pond. It was bright afternoon. The view of that pond revived the old memories in his mind how he used to spend hours after hour in buffalo's company. He approached her and accepted **his** mistake. The buffalo too was in the mood of making amends. She expressed her sorrow that her tail hurt him. Thus the two old friends started living together again and became an example of a unique co-existence. They often used to say, "**We** are friends again. **Our** understanding is better now."

Now let us discuss in detail.

Definition- A pronoun is a word which is used in place of a noun.

Example- Seema is my sister. She has not come here today.

In the above sentence Seema is a noun. In the second sentence word '**she**' is used in place of 'Seema' .This word 'she' is a pronoun.

Kinds of pronoun-

1. Personal pronouns-A personal pronoun is a pronoun that refers to a particular person, group or thing.

I	the speaker, first person
We	Speakers when they are two or more than two., first person
You	second person
They	plural second person
He	male singular ,third person
She	female singular, third person
It	for a baby, animal or non-living thing, singular third person

2. Reflexive Pronoun- Reflexive pronoun is made by adding -self to my, your, him, her, it and selves to our ,your ,them .In such pronouns action done by the subject turns back (reflects)upon it(the subject).

Example: himself, herself, themselves.

He hurt himself.
 She prepared herself.
They dressed themselves.

3. Emphatic Pronoun- To emphasize on the doer of the action –self/-selves is added to the pronoun. Such pronouns are called emphatic pronouns.

Examples:

I will do it myself.
You will practice yourself.
He himself saw it.
We can do it ourselves.
The city itself is not polluted.
The teacher himself told it.

4. Demonstrative Pronoun-These pronouns point to the object they refer so they are called demonstrative Pronouns.

This, that, these, those, such are demonstrative pronouns.

This refers to what is close at hand and nearest to the speaker; that refers to what is 'over there', farther away, and more remote. These and those are plural from of this and that respectively.

This is a grammar book.
This pen is better than that.
That is the India Gate.
These mangoes are cheap.
Those castles are very old.

I may have hurt you but such was not my wish.
My views are different from those of the Chairman.

5. Indefinite Pronoun- When we talk about persons or things in general way but do not refer to them in particular, we use indefinite pronoun.

Such pronouns are words which replace nouns without specifying which noun they replace.

Examples:

Someone has switched off the fan.
Many of them come here.
One hardly stays here for more than five days.
None of his stories are published.
Nobody entered the room.
They say that Saraswati river was in existence.
Somebody has taken away my umbrella.
Few know about it.
Any person may come here.
Everybody must obey the rule.
Always try to help **others.**

6. Distributive Pronoun-These pronouns refer to person or thing one at a time .They are always singular and are followed by a singular verb. 'each', 'either', 'neither' are distributive pronouns.

Each-Each is used to denote every one of the number of persons or things taken together.

Either-Either means the one or the other of two.

Neither- 'Neither' means not the one nor the other of two. It is the negative of either.

Examples: Each of the boys received the award.
              Each girl brought a bag.
              Each student was given an admit card.

41

Either boy got a pen.

These toys cost sixty rupees each.

I sold those kites for five rupees each.

Neither of them was here.

7. Interrogative Pronoun-These pronouns are used for asking questions. Which, who, what are interrogative pronouns.

Examples: Who was speaking?

Where was he going?

Whose is this bag?

Who is sitting there?

Who are you?

Which do you prefer, tea or cold drink?

What is the matter?

What will be their answer?

8. Relative Pronoun-Relative pronoun refers or relates to some noun going before, which is called its antecedent.

Examples-   I met Ram who had just come back.

He has found the pen which I lost.

Here is the file that you gave me.

In the first example 'who' refers to Ram (noun), therefore does the work of a pronoun. The word 'who' connects two sentences- I met Ram. Ram had just come back. It therefore does the work of a conjunction. Thus a relative pronoun may be called a conjunction pronoun. However it is called relative pronoun as like in this example 'who' is relative pronoun because it relates to the noun (Ram) going before, which is called its antecedent.

9. Impersonal Pronoun- These pronouns are used for such nouns which do not have proper names. 'It' and 'they' are such impersonal pronouns.

For example-   It is raining. (It= water)

It is blowing hard.(It = wind)

It is 8o'clock. (It = time)

They say Mr. Ram is honest. (They = people)

10. Reciprocal Pronoun- We use reciprocal pronouns when each of two or more subjects are acting in the same way towards the other.

Example- each other, one another
Raj and Teena are taking care of each other.
Seema and John each other. They are congratulating one another.
We took phone number and email addresses of one another.

Cases of a pronoun

The pronoun may be used in three cases. When it is used as a subject, its case is called subjective case. Its form changes slightly when it is used in possessive case .For example: I am Raj. This is my book.

In the same way when we put any pronoun in place of an object in a sentence its case is called objective case.

For example: He is Raj. I gave <u>him</u> Ten rupees.

Nominative case	Possessive Case	Objective Case	Reflexive case
I	my, mine	me	myself
We	our, ours	us	ourselves
You	your, yours	you	yourself/yourselves
They	their, theirs	them	themselves
He	his	him	himself
She	her, hers	her	herself
It	its	it	itself
Who	whose	Whom	-

One	one's	one	oneself

Number of a pronoun

A pronoun may be singular or plural. The list of personal pronouns in their singular and plural forms in all three cases is as given below:

		Nominative	Objective	Possessive
First person	Singular	I	me	my, mine
	Plural	We	us	our, ours
Second person	Singular	You	you	your, yours
	Plural	You	you	your, yours
Third person	Singular	He, she, it	Him ,her ,it	his ,her/hers, its
	Plural	they	them	their/ theirs

Practice A

Fill the suitable relative pronoun in the blanks.

1. The boy ……. comes here every day is my friend.
2. This is the book …..I got as a gift.
3. She has found the ring………she had lost
4. One …….. tells lies is not believed by anybody.

Practice B

Fill in the blanks with suitable interrogative pronoun-

1. …………….chocolate do you like?
2 …………….is the name of your city?
3. …………..brings milk in your home?

4. …………did you meet on Sunday?

Practice C
Identify the personal pronoun in the given sentences-
1. I have no time to talk to you.
2. Elizabeth does not know what she should do.
3. The bank clerks are sitting there. You should talk to them about the account.
4. The dog is hungry. You should give it something to eat.

Practice D
Identify the emphatic and reflexive pronoun in the sentences given below-
1. You cannot do it yourself.
2. He blamed himself for in.
3. They have benefitted themselves only.
4. The horse hit itself.
5. She herself bought the cream from the mall.
6. The man himself is responsible for his actions.
7. The students work itself is the proof of their excellence.
8. Don't worry. We shall take care of ourselves.

Practice E
Fill in the blanks with personal pronoun as done in the example.
Example: They like to play volleyball. This volleyball is for them.
1. Mary likes chocolate. This chocolate is for (she) …………………………
2. Rohit needs some postcards. These postcards are for …………………
3. My friends like watching movies. These Movie CDs are for …………
4. I know you like mangoes. These mangoes are for…………………………

Practice F
1. Where is Rita? Have you seen ……………
2. That boy is making a lot of noise. Please go and ask ……………to be quiet.

3. I want to invite them in the party. Are..........busy today?

4. I am searching for my book. Have you seen...............?

5. That girl is new in the class. You should help...............

Answers:

Practice A. 1.who, 2.which, 3.which, 4.who

Practice B. 1. Which 2.what 3.who 4.whom

Practice C. 1. I, you 2.she 3.you, them, 4.you, it

Practice D. Reflexive Pronoun –sentences 2,3,4,8

  Emphatic Pronoun – sentences 1,5,6,7

Practice E 1.her 2.him, 3. them 4 you

Practice F 1.her 2.him 3. they 4. it 5.her

Now read again the story given in the beginning of this section '2.2 Pronoun' and see how various kinds of pronouns are used.

2.3 Adjective

Let us begin with a story.

Once there lived a **huge crocodile** in a river. He was **young and sturdy.** There was a **steel bridge** on the river through which many trains passed every day. The **long and broad shadow** of the bridge fell on the river. The crocodile used to come under the shadow and thought that the nature had made this **special arrangement** of shadow for him only. He thought the bridge to be a **long and broad roof**. He felt very proud. A **broad smile** appeared on his face whenever he came under the bridge. His **uneven body** wished to dance and he used to wave his **long tail** in happiness. He lifted his face **slightly high** and made a sound to express his joy. Whenever **any train** passed through the bridge the whole surrounding filled with the **mechanical noise** of the train. The **entire bridge** shook a little and its vibration was felt in nearby area.

The crocodile thought that it was applause by the people sitting on the **moving train** who were happy to see the crocodile suddenly.

Soon a **maintenance work** started on the **railway track** a few kilometers away from the bridge. The passage of trains from the bridge was stopped for **a few days**. The route of the trains was diverted. Now the crocodile was **unhappy**. He thought that his popularity is going down and people no longer want to see him. He shed **crocodile tears** and remained hidden in a cove inside river for many days. Then one day he heard the **same sound** of **passing train** again. He came out on the surface of water and saw the passing train. Then some liquid fell on his body. It was some **sticky juice** that some passenger had thrown after drinking most of it. Some part of the liquid entered in the mouth of the crocodile. He liked the **sweet taste** of that juice. It was **better** than anything that he had tasted till then.He became happy again. He believed that the people have not forgotten him and they love him so much that they have started bringing some **tasty foodstuff** for him to make him happy.

Definition –Adjectives are words which tell something about a noun or pronoun and modify them.

These words describe noun or pronoun (what kind of), they tell their quantity and they identify them (which one?)

Ex. She was buying a green shirt.

Here green is an adjective as it is describing the noun shirt by answering the question what kind of shirt.

Ex. There are 30 students in this class.

Here thirty is also an adjective as it is telling the number of noun 'students'.

Adjectives have four special qualities-

1. Mostly they are used in two ways **(a) attributive use (b) Predicative.**

47

Attributive use –When an adjective is used before a noun and modifies it. When we say- 'Rajkumar is a senior leader.' Or 'He was the best player' it is **attributive use** of adjective 'senior' and 'best'.

Example-Chief secretary, Prime minister, Head master, Former Governor , Late Shri Chandra shekhar

Predicative Use- The use of adjective is predicative when an adjective is used after a noun and modifies it. Adjective comes as a complement of a helping verb.

When we say- 'His decision is uncertain.' or 'This shirt is dirty.' It is **predicative use** of adjective 'uncertain' and 'dirty'.

Example-
It is easy. It is uncertain.
He was proud. They are jealous.
She feels tired. This is very easy.
You are handsome. This problem is difficult to solve.
Raj is ready.

2. Mostly adjectives can be modified by adjectives of degree.

 For example- very simple, quite ordinary , Little slow, highly diligent , rather surprising, rather hard, very easy , fairly modern, slightly heavy, considerably tall, a great deal hot, a bit slower, slightly costly etc.

3. Adjectives have comparative and superlative forms.

Positive Degree	Comparative Degree	Superlative Degree
Good	better	best
Tall	taller	tallest
Much	more	most

4. Many adjectives are made from nouns by adding some suffix.

Ex. Child – childish   fool-foolish   luck-lucky
Emotion –emotional   center –central   hill-hilly

Devotion – devotional	Care-careful	harm-harmful
beauty-beautiful	Care-careless	price-priceless
Effort-effortless	Wood-wooden	gold-golden
Talk –talkative	create-creative	punish-punitive

Kinds of Adjective-Adjectives are of 10 kinds:

1. Adjective of quality-- These adjective are used to describe the nature and characteristics of a noun/pronoun .They answer the question 'what kind'.

Holy,naughty,small,big,hot,cold,good,bad,beautiful,ugly,handsome,careful ,ignorant,watchful,alert,active, intelligent, miser, diligent, wise, tasty, healthy, nutritious, honest .

Ex.

He is handsome.
She is a pretty girl.
Delhi is a historical city.
Her frock is white**.**

2. Adjective of Quantity-These adjectives help to show the amount of the noun/pronoun. They answer the question 'how much'.

Some, more, little, a little, all, a lot, enough, none, much, half, most, no, enough, great, any

Ex. I want some milk.
  They have enough money.
  All the milk was used in making coffee.
  He has completed most of the projects.

3. Adjective of number- These adjectives are used to describe the number of a noun/pronoun and their place in an order.

They fall under two broad categories-Indefinite Numeral Adjective and Definite Numeral Adjectives.

A)Definite Numeral Adjectives –These adjectives tell the definite number of nouns.

I have ten rupees.
She needs ten potatoes.
There are eleven players in a cricket team.
This category may be subdivided into following categories:
Cardinals- One, Two, three, four, five etc.
Ordinals-first, second, third, fourth etc.
Multiplicative- single, double, triple, twice, thrice, fourfold, fivefold etc.
Fractional - half, one-third, one-fourth etc.

B] Indefinite Numeral Adjectives- These adjectives do not tell definite number of a noun.

Example-
Many leaders came to attend the meeting.
They have enough money.
Raj has some books in his bag.
Few people use smart card to buy grain.
He has a lot of old stamps in his collection.

4. Demonstrative adjective-The adjective which point out or indicate a particular noun or pronoun are called demonstrative adjective.

Example-this, that, these, those, such
Ex. I can carry that bag.
    Rohit can take these fruits.

5. Distributive adjective- An adjective that is used to refer to each and every person or thing out of a group/collection separately is called distributive adjective.

Example-Each, every, Either, neither

Every student has a scholar number.
Every room is locked.
Each girl will get shoes.
Either book is useful.
Neither boy brought any bat.

6. Interrogative adjective-What, whose, which and where are used with noun/pronoun to ask questions .These are called interrogative adjective.

Example-   Which place will you visit this year?
            Whose shirt is the brightest?
            What color do you like?
            Where was Deepa going?
            Which shirt did she buy?
            Whose name was suggested?

7. Possessive Adjective-When words like 'my', 'your', 'their', 'our', 'his', 'her', 'its' are used immediately before nouns, then these are called possessive adjectives.

Example- This is my book. He can use your bike. They have taken his pen. I will ask for her advice. We shall go in our car. They have removed their support.

8. Proper Adjective-The adjectives which are formed by proper nouns are called proper adjectives.

Example- Indian, Australian, English, Spanish, Americans, Canadians

9. Exclamatory Adjective-When the word 'what' is used as an adjective to express any strong feeling it is called exclamatory adjective.

Example-   What a pleasant surprise!

<u>What</u> a shocking news you have given!

<u>What</u> an unexpected result he has produced!

10. Emphasizing Adjective-When words 'own' and 'vary' are used to emphasize on any person or thing ,they are called emphasizing adjectives.

Example-   I am using my <u>own</u> laptop.

He is the <u>very</u> person who created this garden.

It was our <u>own </u>decision.

Degrees of adjectives-

We can compare a noun or pronoun with another noun or pronoun. For example if a boy Raj is 5 feet tall and another boy Anil is 4 feet tall then we can say that Raj is taller than Anil. We can say it in another way that Anil is shorter than Raj. Here we have used **comparative degree** of adjective –taller and shorter. This degree is used to compare two nouns or pronouns.

Superlative degree is used to describe the superiority or the extreme of a quality found in any object or person .For example if a boy Shivam is so tall that no other boy in the class is as tall as he is ,then we say that 'Shivam is the tallest boy of the class.'

The following list shows three degrees of some adjectives.

The comparative and superlative degrees are made by addine '-er' and '–est' respectively in the positive degree. If there is 'e' in the end of the adjective than only '–r' and '-st' are added to make other two degrees.

Positive degree	Comparative degree	Superlative degree
Cheap	cheaper	Cheapest
Bold	bolder	boldest
bitter	bitterer	bitterest
brief	briefer	briefest
clean	cleaner	cleanest
cheap	cheaper	cheapest

calm	calmer	calmest
clever	cleverer	cleverest
cold	colder	coldest
cute	cuter	cutest
dark	darker	darkest
dear	dearer	dearest
deep	deeper	deepest
fast	faster	fastest
few	fewer	fewest
great	greater	greatest
grand	grander	grandest
high	higher	highest
hard	harder	hardest
keen	keener	keenest
kind	kinder	kindest
light	lighter	lightest
Long	longer	longest
low	lower	lowest
narrow	narrower	Narrowest
near	nearer	nearest
nice	nicer	nicest
old	older	oldest
proud	prouder	proudest
poor	poorer	poorest
pleasant	pleasanter	pleasantest
pure	purer	purest
quiet	quieter	quietest
rich	richer	richest
rough	rougher	roughest
safe	safer	Safest
small	smaller	smallest
sweet	sweeter	sweetest
strong	strongest	strongest
Short	shorter	Shortest
smart	smarter	smartest
thick	thicker	thickest
vain	vainer	vainest
weak	weak	weakest
Wide	wider	Widest

Warm	warmer	warmest
young	younger	youngest

In some adjectives comparative and superlative degrees are made by putting more and most/less and least before them.

Accurate	More accurate	Most accurate
dangerous	More dangerous	Most dangerous
Handsome	More handsome	Most handsome
Attractive	More attractive	Most attractive
Delicious	More delicious	Most delicious
Useful	More useful	Most useful
Modern	More modern	Most modern
Patient	More patient	Most patient
Interesting	More interesting	Most interesting
Brilliant	less brilliant	least brilliant
Careless	less careless	least careless
Honest	less honest	least honest
Powerful	less powerful	least powerful

If any adjective ends in 'y' then we can make their comparative and superlative degree in this way:

1. If there is a consonant before 'y': 'y' is removed and '-ier', '-iest' are added to make other two degree.

2. If there is a vowel before 'y': 'y' is not removed .Just '-er' and '-est' are added after 'y' to make other two degrees

Busy	busier	busiest
Cozy	cozier	coziest
Dry	drier	driest
Happy	Happier	Happiest
Heavy	heavier	heaviest
Noisy	noisier	Noisiest
Easy	easier	Easiest
Lazy	lazier	Laziest

Merry	merrier	merriest
Pretty	Prettier	Prettiest
Ugly	uglier	ugliest
gay	gayer	gayest
grey	greyer	greyest

Some adjectives do not follow any of the above rules to make comparative and superlative degrees:

Good	Better	best
bad	worse	Worst
much	more	most
far	farther	Farthest
in	inner	innermost
little	less, lesser	least
late	later, latter	latest, last
nigh	nigher	nighest
up	upper	uppermost, upmost

If there is any vowel just before the ending letter of an adjective ,we make comparative and superlative degree by writing the last letter twice before adding –er and-est.

big	bigger	biggest
fat	fatter	fattest
fit	fitter	fittest
hot	hotter	hottest
mad	madder	maddest
sad	sadder	saddest
thin	thinner	thinnest
wet	wetter	wettest

A list of some commonly used adjectives is given below for ready reference of the reader-

Abundant,accurate,addicted,adventurous,adorable,afraid,aggressive,alert,aloof,ambitious,ancient,angry,annoying,anuxious,arrogant,ashamed, attractive,auspicious,awful,bad,beneficial,bitter,black,boring,bright, broad, broken ,busy, calm, capable, careless , caring ,cautious, charming, cheap ,dirty, delicate, determined ,delicious, dusty, early, efficient, elegant, empty , enthusiastic ,excellent ,exciting ,expensive ,fabulous ,famous, fancy, fantastic, fast ,fearful, friendly ,fearful ,foolish ,filthy ,fertile ,fearless ,funny ,gentle ,glamorous, glorious, gorgeous, graceful, grateful, great ,greedy ,green ,handsome ,happy, harsh ,healthy, heavy ,helpful, hilarious, historical, horrible, hot ,huge ,hungry ,ignorant ,illegal, imaginary, important ,impossible, innocent, intelligent , interesting ,jealous, jolly, juicy, juvenile ,kind ,legal, large ,light, literate, little, lively, lonely, loud, lovely, lucky ,magical ,magnificent ,massive, mature ,mean ,modern, narrow ,nasty, naughty, nervous, new ,nutritious ,obedient ,obese ,obnoxious, old ,peaceful , pink, polite ,poor, powerful ,precious ,pretty, proud, quick, quiet ,rapid, rare, red, remarkable, rich ,responsible, romantic, royal ,rude ,scintillating, secretive, selfish ,serious, sharp ,shiny ,shocking, short, shy ,silly ,sincere ,skinny ,,slim ,slow small, soft ,spicy ,spiritual ,splendid, strong,, successful, sweet, talented ,tall ,tasty, tense, terrible, thick ,thin, tiny, ugly, unique, untidy, upset ,victorious, violent, vulgar, warm, weak, wealthy ,wide, wise ,witty ,wonderful, worried ,young, youthful ,jealous , zigzag.

Practice 1(Adjectives)

Use suitable form of the words in brackets (comparative /superlative) to fill the blank.

a. My house is …….…….than yours.(bigger/big)
b. This flower is……..…….than that flower.(beautiful)
c. This is the …….……..…..book I have ever read.(interesting)
d. Non smokers usually live……..…..than smokers.(long)
e. Which is the…………..…... animal in the world.(dangerous)
f. A holiday by the sea is……….than a holiday in the mountains. (good)
g. It is strange but often a coke is ……….than a beer. (expensive)
h. Who is the………..…….woman on the earth.(rich)

i. The weather this summer is ....than last summer.(bad)

j. He was the ....thief of all.(clever

Practice 2

Complete the following sentences with the correct comparative form of the adjective.

[Heavy, important, quiet, healthy, easy, better, cheap, thin, expensive, difficult, crowded]

(i)   I think that good health is ....than money.

(ii)   I can't carry my bag, it's much ....than yours.

(iii)   You look ....than the last time we saw you. Have you been sick?

(iv)   I couldn't get a seat in the train .It was ....than usual.

(v)   A car is ....than a bike.

(vi)   I can't understand this lesson. It is ....than the last one.

(vii)   I can't study in this noisy room. I'm going to find ....place.

(viii) Orange juice is ....than Limka .

(ix)   There is a great sale today. Televisions are 20% ....than before.

(x)   The doctor told me that I can go back to work if I feel ....tomorrow.

Practice 3

Make your own comparisons using the words provided and the structure given below-

Ex.- My house /big/yours   My house is bigger than yours.

My pen/expensive /your pen   My pen is not as expensive as your pen.

(i)   History /interesting /Geography

        …………………………………………………

(ii)   Train/fast/airplane…………………………………

(iii)   Mango/sweet/guava…………………………………

(iv)   Morning/bright/afternoon……………………………

(v)   Sparrow/small/crow…………………………………

(vi)   Car/expensive/motorcycle……………………………

Practice 4

Fill in the blanks with comparative or superlative degree of adjective.

a. He works …………………than you.(hard/harder/the hardest)

b. Dinesh is …………………boy in the class.(tall/taller/the taller)

c. Mt.Everest is ………mountain peak in the world.(high/higher/the highest)

d. This pen is ………..than your pen .(cheap/cheaper/the cheapest)

e. He is ……………...students in the class. (intelligent/more intelligent/most intelligent)

f. Anil is not so tall. He is ……………….than Deepak. (short/shorter/the shortest)

g. Rajiv Gandhi was ……………Prime minister of India. (young/younger/the youngest)

Practice 5

Make comparisons of the following. Write three sentences for each set. Use positive, comparative and superlative degree to compare them as given in the example.

Example- cherry, guava, melon

    a.   Cherry is not as big as guava.

    b.   Guava is bigger than cherry.

    c.   Melon is biggest fruit of the three.

       1. Car, truck, bike--------------------------heavy

       2. Purse, bag, suitcase-----------------------small

3. Cotton, wood, Aluminum-------------------heavy
4. Ice, water, vapour--------------------------- light
5. Letter, telegram, e-mail-------------------fast

Practice6.

Write the nouns and adjectives used in these sentences in the correct columns of the table given below-

1. Do you like Italian food?
2. We sat at the kitchen table and ate dinner.
3. Grammar is an interesting subject.
4. I have a red grammar book.
5. We bought a beautiful cup in China.
6. She has an important job in the police department.

Table:

adjectives	Nouns used as adjectives	nouns

Order of adjectives

In English it is common to use more than one adjective to describe a noun .These adjectives must be used in the proper order.

Example-Here is a beautiful red cloth flag.
        Why does beautiful come before red?
        Why does red come before cloth?

We use the following table to practice using the proper order of adjectives in the sentences.

OPINION	SIZE	SHAPE	AGE	COLOUR	NATIONALITY	MATERIAL

Examples-a nice beautiful young lady, a big red German car, a dangerous tall black bull

Practice 7

Choose the correct order of adjectives in the following sentences-

(i).The woman is wearing a ....dress.
a. yellow long   b. long yellow
(ii)He is a.............man
a. tall thin   b. thin tall
(iii)The company makes ....products.
a. excellent farming   b. farming excellent
iv)The scientists have found a..............cure for disease.
a. new great   b .great new
v) The.............. woman did well on the test.
a. intelligent young   b. young intelligent

Answers:

Practice 1 a. bigger, b. more beautiful, c. most interesting d. longer e. most dangerous f. better g. more expensive h. richest i. worse j. cleverest

Practice 2 (i) more important (ii)heavier (iii)thinner (iv)more crowded (v)more expensive (vi)more difficult (vii)quieter (viii)healthier (ix)cheaper (x)better

Practice 3 (i) History is more interesting than Geography.

(ii)An Airplane is faster than a train.

(iii) Mango is sweeter than guava.

(iv)An afternoon is brighter than a morning.

(v) Sparrows are smaller than crows.

(vi)A Car is more expensive than a motorcycle.

Practice 4 a. harder, b. the tallest, c. the highest d. cheaper e. the most intelligent, f. shorter, g. the youngest

Practice 5:1 a.A bike is not as heavy as a car.

b. A car is heavier than a bike.

c. A truck is heaviest vehicle of the three.

2. Same as 1.Apply the same method.

Practice6:

adjectives	Nouns used as adjectives	nouns
Italian		food
	kitchen	Table ,dinner
interesting		Subject, grammar
red	grammar	book
beautiful		Cup, China
important	police	job

Practice7 (i) long yellow (ii)tall thin (iii)excellent farming (iv)great new (v)intelligent young

2.4 Verb

Let us begin with a story:

The Red Fort,which **has been** the epitome of power for the Mughals ,the British and the free India, **was built** by Emperor Shah Jahan in 1639.**Sustaining** its position as the symbol of power through centuries, it **was** here that the national flag **was hoisted** for the first time after Independence.

The Octagonal fort **encloses** its elegant buildings in a two-mile-long, 70 feet high and 45 feet wide walls. The fort **has** a 75-feet wide and 30 feet deep moat on three sides while the river Yamuna surrounds it on the forth. The fort **has** two entrances-one through the Delhi gate, originally called Akbarabadi Darwaza, and the other through Lahore Gate. The Delhi Gate **leads** to Jama Masjid through Faiz Bazaar with the Lahore Gate being its principal entrance.

On entering the Lahore Gate, one **comes across** a 270 feet long arcade, which **has** small shops on both sides where one can pick up souvenirs. This is Meena Bazaar,the erstwhile principal shopping centre of Shah Jahan's nobles.

Further ahead, **is** the Jilau Khana with its sides lined with rooms meant for guards and their superintendents. On the extreme end **stands** the Drum House, called the naqqar Khana or Naubat Khana, used **to regulate** the entry of visitors into the fort. The first floor **was** a stage for musicians, who **welcomed** royal visitors.

A word or group of words that expresses an action (such as eat), an event (such as happen) or a state (such as exist) is called a verb. [Oxford Advanced Learners Dictionary]

Kinds of Verb- There are six types of verbs.

1. Transitive Verb
2. Intransitive Verb
3. Verbs of incomplete Predication
4. Auxiliary Verb
5. Impersonal Verb

6. Prepositional Verb

1. Transitive Verb- Those verbs which are not limited to subject only but affect the other person or thing also are called transitive verb. The person or thing that is affected by verb is called its object. Thus every transitive verb has its object.

Example- Suresh eats a mango.

Here verb 'eat' is not limited to Suresh only but affects a mango, so 'eat' is a transitive verb.

2. Intransitive Verb-   These verbs do not have their direct object.

Example-   The sheep walk in groups.
                They run on the road.
                He goes.
                She comes by train.
                Geeta dances on the stage.

3. Verbs of incomplete Predication- The verb which need some other words to complete their meaning are called verbs of incomplete predication. Verbs is, was, will be etc. are such verbs which need other words to complete their meaning.

Example- He is an actor. Your uncle was an engineer.

Here **is** and **was** verbs need words actor and engineer to complete the meaning .So these verbs are called verbs of incomplete predication.

These verbs are of two types-

a)When the meaning of any intransitive verb is incomplete without a supplement word then that verb is called **intransitive verb of incomplete predication**.

Examples- He is my cousin. Gopal became impatient. The girl seems hungry. It grew very cold. You appear very tired. Akbar was a great Emperor. They are sad.

b)When any transitive verb's meaning is not complete even with the object and another supplement word is required to complete its meaning ,then such a verb is called **transitive verb with incomplete predication.**

Examples-   The players decided Rohit their captain.
                  He considers it useless.
                  They thought you a fool.
                  They would choose her their leader.

4. Auxiliary Verb-Those verbs which come before main verb and help in making its tense or mood are called auxiliary verb.

Examples-

Ram has opened the shop. **(**Auxiliary verb 'has' is used before main verb' opened')

Your shirt is drying. (Auxiliary verb 'is' is used before main verb' drying')

She will help me. (auxiliary verb 'will' is used before main verb 'help')

[Note-Auxiliary verb becomes main verb when it is the only verb used in a sentence. For example- The girl is honest. He has a box.]

5.Impersonal Verb-When ' it' and 'they' are used as subject to describe an event, weather or distance etc., the verb coming after these is called impersonal verb.

Example-It is raining. It is nine o'clock. They say dark clouds bring rain. It is five miles from here**.**

6. Prepositional Verb-Some verbs come with preposition and act as transitive verbs. Such verbs are called prepositional verbs.

Example- You must act on his advice. They believe in honesty. The king was overcome by enemy.

Three forms of the verb

Regular verb- A verb that forms its past tense and past participle by adding –d or –ed (or in some cases –t) to the base form.

Present/Infinitive Form	Past Form	Past Participle Form
Abuse	abused	abused
Act	acted	acted
Add	added	added
Admire	admired	admired
Advise	advised	advised
afford	afforded	afforded
agree	agreed	agreed
alert	alerted	alerted
allow	allowed	allowed
amuse	amused	amused
analyse	analysed	analysed
announce	announced	announced
annoy	annoyed	annoyed
Answer	answered	answered
appologise	appologised	appologised
Appear	appeared	appeared
Appoint	appointed	appointed
appreciate	appreciated	appreciated
approve	approved	approved
argue	argued	argued
arrange	arranged	arranged
arrest	arrested	arrested
arrive	arrived	arrived
Ask	Asked	Asked
attach	attached	attached
attack	attacked	attacked
attempt	attempted	attempted
attend	attended	attended
attract	attracted	attracted
avoid	avoided	avoided
Back	backed	backed

Bake	baked	baked
Balance	balanced	balanced
Ban	banned	banned
Bang	banged	banged
Bare	bared	bared
Bat	batted	batted
Bark	barked	barked
Bathe	bathed	bathed
Battle	Battled	Battled
Beam	Beamed	Beamed
beg	begged	begged
Behave	Behaved	Behaved
Belong	Belonged	Belonged
Bleach	Bleached	Bleached
Bless	Blessed	Blessed
Blind	Blinded	Blinded
Blink	Blinked	Blinked
Blot	Blotted	Blotted
Blush	Blushed	Blushed
Boast	Boasted	Boasted
Boil	Boiled	Boiled
Bolt	Bolted	Bolted
Bomb	Bombed	Bombed
Book	Booked	booked
Bore	Bored	bored
Borrow	Borrowed	Borrowed
Bounce	bounced	Bounced
Bow	bowed	bowed
Box	boxed	boxed
Branch	Branched	Branched
Breathe	breathed	breathed
Bruise	bruised	bruised
Brush	brushed	brushed
Bubble	bubbled	bubbled
Bump	bumped	bumped
Bury	buried	buried
Buzz	buzzed	buzzed
Calculate	calculated	calculated
call	called	called

camp	camped	camped
care	cared	cared
carry	carried	carried
carve	carved	carved
cause	caused	caused
challenge	challenged	challenged
change	changed	changed
charge	charged	charged
chase	chased	chased
cheat	cheated	cheated
check	checked	checked
cheer	cheered	cheered
chew	chewed	chewed
choke	choked	choked
chop	chopped	chopped
claim	claimed	claimed
clap	clapped	clapped
clean	cleaned	cleaned
clear	cleared	cleared
clip	clipped	clipped
close	closed	closed
coach	coached	coached
coil	coiled	coiled
collect	collected	collected
colour	coloured	coloured
comb	combed	combed
command	commanded	commanded
communicate	communicated	communicated
compare	compared	compared
compete	completed	completed
complain	complained	complained
complete	completed	completed
concentrate	concentrated	concentrated
concern	concerned	concerned
confess	confessed	confessed
confuse	confused	confused
connect	connected	connected
consider	considered	considered
consist	consisted	consisted

contain	contained	contained
continue	continued	continued
copy	copied	copied
correct	corrected	corrected
cough	coughed	coughed
count	counted	counted
cover	covered	covered
crack	cracked	cracked
crash	crashed	crashed
crawl	crawled	crawled
cross	crossed	crossed
crush	crushed	crushed
cry	cried	cried
cure	cured	cured
curve	curved	curved
cycle	cycled	cycled
damage	damaged	damaged
dance	danced	danced
dare	dared	dared
decay	decayed	decayed
deceive	deceived	deceived
decide	decided	decided
decorate	decorate	decorated
delay	delayed	delayed
delight	delighted	delighted
deliver	delivered	delivered
disarm	disarmed	disarmed
discover	discovered	discovered
dislike	disliked	disliked
divide	divided	divided
double	doubled	doubled
doubt	doubted	doubted
drag	dragged	dragged
drain	drained	drained
dream	dreamed	dreamed
dress	dressed	dressed
drip	dripped	dripped
drop	dropped	dropped
drown	drowned	drowned

drum	drummed	drummed
dry	dried	dried
dust	dusted	dusted
earn	earned	earned
educate	educated	educated
embarrass	embarrassed	embarrassed
employ	employed	employed
empty	emptied	emptied
encourage	encouraged	encouraged
end	ended	ended
enjoy	enjoyed	enjoyed
enter	entered	entered
entertain	entertained	entertained
escape	escaped	escaped
examine	examined	examined
excite	excited	excited
excuse	excused	excused
exercise	exercised	exercised
exist	existed	existed
expand	expanded	expanded
expect	expected	expected
explain	explained	explained
extend	extended	extended
face	faced	faced
fade	faded	faded
fail	failed	failed
fancy	fancied	fancied
fasten	fastened	fastened
fax	faxed	faxed
fear	feared	feared
fence	fenced	fenced
fetch	fetched	fetched
file	filed	filed
fill	filled	filled
film	filmed	filmed
fire	fired	fired
fit	fitted	fitted
fix	fixed	fixed
flap	flapped	flapped

flash	flashed	flashed
float	floated	floated
flood	flooded	flooded
flow	flowed	flowed
flower	flowered	flowered
fold	folded	folded
follow	followed	followed
fool	fooled	fooled
force	forced	forced
form	formed	formed
found	founded	founded
frame	framed	framed
frighten	frightened	frightened
fry	fried	fried
gather	gathered	gathered
gaze	gazed	gazed
glow	glowed	glowed
glue	glued	glued
grab	grabbed	grabbed
grate	grated	grated
grease	greased	greased
greet	greeted	greeted
grin	grinned	grinned
grip	gripped	gripped
groan	groaned	groaned
guarantee	guaranteed	guaranteed
guard	guarded	guarded
guess	guessed	guessed
guide	guided	guided
hammer	hammered	hammered
hand	handed	handed
handle	handled	handled
hang	hanged	hanged
happen	happened	happened
harass	harassed	harassed
harm	harmed	harmed
hate	hated	hated
haunt	haunted	haunted
head	headed	headed

heal	healed	healed
heap	heaped	heaped
heat	heated	heated
help	helped	helped
hook	hooked	hooked
hop	hopped	hopped
hope	hoped	hoped
hover	hovered	hovered
hug	hugged	hugged
hum	hummed	hummed
hunt	hunted	hunted
hurry	hurried	hurried
identify	identified	identified
ignore	ignored	ignored
imagine	imagined	imagined
impress	impressed	impressed
improve	improved	improved
include	included	included
increase	increased	increased
influence	influenced	influenced
inform	informed	informed
inject	injected	injected
injure	injured	injured
instruct	instructed	instructed
intend	intended	intended
interest	interested	interested
interfere	interfered	interfered
interrupt	interrupted	interrupted
introduce	introduced	introduced
invent	invented	invented
invite	invited	invited
irritate	irritated	irritated
itch	itched	itched
jail	jailed	jailed
jog	jogged	jogged
joke	joked	joked
juggle	juggled	juggled
jam	jammed	jammed
join	joined	joined

judge	judged	judged
jump	jumped	jumped
kick	kicked	kicked
kill	killed	killed
kiss	kissed	kissed
kneel	kneeled	kneeled
knit	knitted	knitted
knock	knocked	knocked
knot	knot	knot
label	labeled	labeled
learn	learned	learned
lighten	lightened	lightened
load	loaded	loaded
land	landed	landed
last	lasted	lasted
laugh	laughed	laughed
launch	launched	launched
level	leveled	leveled
license	licensed	licensed
lick	licked	licked
lie	lied	lied
like	liked	liked
list	listed	listed
listen	listened	listened
live	lived	lived
lock	locked	locked
long	longed	longed
look	looked	looked
love	loved	loved
man	manned	manned
manage	managed	managed
march	marched	marched
mark	marked	marked
marry	married	married
match	matched	matched
mate	mated	mated
matter	mattered	mattered
measure	measured	measured
meddle	meddled	meddled

melt	melted	melted
memorize	memorized	memorized
mend	mended	mended
mess up	messed up	messed up
milk	milked	milked
mine	mined	mined
miss	missed	missed
mix	mixed	mixed
moan	moaned	moaned
moor	moored	moored
mourn	mourned	mourned
move	moved	moved
muddle	muddled	muddled
mug	mugged	mugged
multiply	multiplied	multiplied
murder	murdered	murdered
nail	nailed	nailed
name	named	named
need	needed	needed
nest	nested	nested
nod	nodded	nodded
note	noted	noted
notice	noticed	noticed
number	numbered	numbered
obey	obeyed	obeyed
object	objected	objected
observe	observed	observed
obtain	obtained	obtained
occur	occurred	occurred
offend	offended	offended
offer	offered	offered
open	opened	opened
order	ordered	ordered
overflow	overflowed	overflowed
owe	owed	owed
own	owned	owned
pack	packed	packed
paddle	paddled	paddled
paint	painted	painted

park	parked	parked
part	parted	parted
pass	passed	passed
paste	pasted	pasted
pat	patted	patted
pause	paused	paused
peck	pecked	pecked
pedal	pedalled	pedaled
peel	peeled	peeled
peep	peeped	peeped
perform	performed	performed
permit	permitted	permitted
phone	phoned	phoned
pick	picked	picked
pinch	pinched	pinched
pine	pined	pined
place	placed	placed
plan	planned	planned
plant	planted	planted
play	played	played
please	pleased	pleased
plug	plugged	plugged
point	pointed	pointed
poke	poked	poked
polish	polished	polished
pop	popped	popped
possess	possessed	possessed
post	posted	posted
pour	poured	poured
practice	practiced	practiced
pray	prayed	prayed
preach	preached	preached
precede	preceded	preceded
prefer	preferred	preferred
prepare	prepared	prepared
present	presented	presented
preserve	preserved	preserved
press	pressed	pressed
pretend	pretended	pretended

prevent	prevented	prevented
prick	pricked	pricked
print	printed	printed
produce	produced	produced
program	programmed	programmed
promise	promised	promised
protect	protected	protected
provide	provided	provided
pull	pulled	pulled
pump	pumped	pumped
punch	punched	punched
puncture	puncture	puncture
punish	punished	punished
push	pushed	pushed
question	questioned	questioned
queue	queued	queued
race	raced	raced
radiate	radiated	radiated
rain	rained	rained
raise	raised	raised
reach	reached	reached
realize	realized	realized
receive	received	received
recognize	recognized	recognized
record	recorded	recorded
reduce	reduced	reduced
reflect	reflected	reflected
refuse	refused	refused
regret	regretted	regretted
reign	reigned	reigned
reject	rejected	rejected
rejoice	rejoiced	rejoiced
relax	relaxed	relaxed
release	released	released
rely	relied	relied
remain	remained	remained
remember	remembered	remembered
remind	reminded	reminded
remove	removed	removed

repair	repaired	repaired
repeat	repeated	repeated
replace	replaced	replaced
reply	replied	replied
report	reported	reported
reproduce	reproduced	reproduced
request	requested	requested
rescue	rescued	rescued
retire	retired	retired
return	returned	returned
rhyme	rhymed	rhymed
rinse	rinsed	rinsed
risk	risked	risked
rob	robbed	robbed
rock	rocked	rocked
roll	rolled	rolled
rot	rotted	rotted
rub	rubbed	rubbed
ruin	ruined	ruined
rule	ruled	ruled
rush	rushed	rushed
sack	sacked	sacked
sail	sailed	sailed
satisfy	satisfied	satisfied
save	saved	saved
saw	sawed	sawed
scare	scared	scared
scatter	scattered	scattered
scold	scolded	scolded
scorch	scorched	scorched
scrape	scrapped	scrapped
scratch	scratched	scratched
scream	screamed	screamed
screw	screwed	screwed
scribble	scribbled	scribbled
scrub	scrubbed	scrubbed
seal	sealed	sealed
search	searched	searched
separate	separated	separated

serve	served	served
settle	settled	settled
shade	shaded	shaded
share	shared	shared
shave	shaved	shaved
shelter	sheltered	sheltered
shop	shopped	shopped
shrug	shrugged	shrugged
sigh	sighed	sighed
sign	signed	signed
signal	signaled	signaled
sin	sinned	sinned
sip	sipped	sipped
ski	skied	skied
skip	skipped	skipped
slap	slapped	slapped
slip	slipped	slipped
slow	slowed	slowed
smash	smashed	smashed
smell	smelled	smelled
smile	smiled	smiled
smoke	smoked	smoked
snatch	snatched	snatched
sneeze	sneezed	sneezed
sniff	sniffed	sniffed
snore	snored	snored
snow	snowed	snowed
soak	soaked	soaked
spare	spared	spared
spark	sparked	sparked
sparkle	sparkled	sparkled
spell	spelled	spelled
spill	spilled	spilled
spoil	spoiled	spoiled
spot	spotted	spotted
spray	sprayed	sprayed
sprout	sprouted	sprouted
squash	squashed	squashed
squeak	squeaked	squeaked

squeal	squealed	squealed
squeeze	squeezed	squeezed
stain	stained	stained
stamp	stamped	stamped
stare	stared	stared
start	started	started
stay	stayed	stayed
steer	steered	steered
step	stepped	stepped
stir	stirred	stirred
stitch	stitched	stitched
strap	strapped	strapped
strengthen	strengthened	strengthened
stretch	stretched	stretched
strip	stripped	stripped
stroke	stroked	stroked
stuff	stuffed	stuffed
subtract	subtracted	subtracted
succeed	succeeded	succeeded
suck	sucked	sucked
suffer	suffered	suffered
suggest	suggested	suggested
suit	suited	suited
supply	supplied	supplied
support	supported	supported
suppose	supposed	supposed
surprise	surprised	surprised
surround	surrounded	surrounded
suspect	suspected	suspected
suspend	suspended	suspended
switch	switched	switched
talk	talked	talked
tame	tamed	tamed
tap	tapped	tapped
taste	tasted	tasted
tease	teased	teased
telephone	telephoned	telephoned
tempt	tempted	tempted
terrify	terrified	terrified

test	tested	tested
thank	thanked	thanked
thaw	thawed	thawed
tick	ticked	ticked
tickle	tickled	tickled
tie	tied	tied
time	timed	timed
tip	tipped	tipped
tire	tired	tired
touch	touched	touched
tour	toured	toured
tow	towed	towed
trace	traced	traced
trade	traded	traded
train	trained	trained
transport	transported	transported
trap	trapped	trapped
travel	traveled	traveled
treat	treated	treated
tremble	trembled	trembled
trick	tricked	tricked
trip	tripped	tripped
trot	trotted	trotted
trouble	troubled	troubled
trust	trusted	trusted
try	tried	tried
tug	tugged	tugged
tumble	tumbled	tumbled
turn	turned	turned
twist	twisted	twisted
type	typed	typed
undress	undressed	undressed
unfasten	unfastened	unfastened
unite	united	united
unlock	unlocked	unlocked
unpack	unpacked	unpacked
untie	untied	untied
use	used	used
vanish	vanished	vanished

visit	visited	visited
wail	wailed	wailed
wait	waited	waited
walk	walked	walked
wander	wandered	wandered
want	wanted	wanted
warm	warmed	warmed
warn	warned	warned
wash	washed	washed
waste	wasted	wasted
watch	watched	watched
water	watered	watered
wave	waved	waved
weigh	weighed	weighed
welcome	welcomed	welcomed
whine	whined	whined
whip	whipped	whipped
whirl	whirled	whirled
whisper	whispered	whispered
whistle	whistled	whistled
wink	winked	winked
wipe	wiped	wiped
wish	wished	wished
wobble	wobbled	wobbled
wonder	wondered	wondered
work	worked	worked
worry	worried	worried
wrap	wrapped	wrapped
wreck	wrecked	wrecked
wrestle	wrestled	wrestled
wriggle	wriggled	wriggled
x-ray	x-rayed	x-rayed
yawn	yawned	yawned
yell	yelled	yelled
zip	zipped	zipped
zoom	zoomed	zoomed

Irregular Verb: A verb that does not follow a regular pattern in making its past form and past participle form. The simple past and past participle forms of irregular verbs can end in a variety of ways, with absolutely no consistent pattern.

Present/Infinitive form	Past form	Past participle form
awake	awoke	awaken
be	was/were	been
beat	beat	beaten
become	became	become
begin	began	begun
bend	bent	bent
bet	bet	bet
bid	bid	bid
bite	bit	bitten
blow	blew	blown
break	broke	broken
bring	brought	brought
broadcast	broadcast	broadcast
build	built	built
burn	burned/burnt	burned/burnt
buy	bought	bought
bring	brought	brought
build	built	built
catch	caught	caught
choose	chose	chosen
come	came	come
cost	cost	cost
cut	cut	cut
dig	dug	dug
do	did	done
draw	drew	drawn
dream	dreamt	dreamt
drink	drank	drunk
drive	drove	driven
eat	ate	eaten
fall	fell	fallen
feed	fed	fed
feel	felt	felt

fight	fought	fought
find	found	found
flow	flew	flown
fly	flew	flown
forget	forgot	forgotten
forgive	forgave	forgiven
freeze	froze	frozen
get	got	got
give	gave	given
go	went	gone
grow	grew	grown
hang	hung	hung
have	had	had
hear	heard	heard
hide	hid	hidden
hit	hit	hit
hold	held	held
hurt	hurt	hurt
keep	kept	kept
knit	knit	knit
know	knew	known
lay	laid	laid
lead	led	led
learn	learned/learnt	learned/learnt
leave	left	left
lend	left	left
let	let	let
lie	lay	lain
lose	lost	lost
make	made	made
mean	meant	meant
meet	met	met
pay	paid	paid
put	put	put
read	read	read
ride	rode	ridden
ring	rang	rung
rise	rose	risen
run	ran	run

say	said	said
see	saw	seen
sell	sold	sold
send	sent	sent
set	set	set
shake	shook	shaken
shoot	shot	shot
show	showed	shown
shrink	shrank	shrunk
shut	shut	shut
sing	sang	sung
sink	sank	sunk
sit	sat	sit
sleep	slept	slept
smell	smelt	smelt
sow	sowed	sown
speak	spoke	spoken
spend	spent	spent
spread	spread	spread
stand	stood	stood
steal	stole	stolen
stick	stuck	stuck
strike	struck	struck
swim	swam	swum
take	took	taken
teach	taught	taught
tear	tore	torn
tell	told	told
think	thought	thought
throw	threw	thrown
understand	understood	understood
wake	woke	woken
wear	wore	worn
win	won	won
write	wrote	written

Practice 1

Classify the following verbs into transitive, intransitive, auxiliary and prepositional verbs:

Take, sing, walk, run, look into, was, drink, will, go, act on, believe in

Practice2

Fill the table with forms of verbs:

Present Form	Past form	Past Participle form
take		
	wrote	
use		
	arrived	
cut		
		drunk
	asked	
		sent

Practice 3

Circle the correct verb or verbs in each sentence.

a. Amit plays cricket.
b. Rajeev and Rohit brought books.
c. A leaf fell from the tree.
d. The moon appears at night.
e. My brother likes to eat chocolate cake.
f. The fruits of this tree are sweet.
g. Will you open the window please?
h. Deepali opened a boutique.
i. They saw the film.
j. I visit him every Sunday.

Practice 4

Circle the verbs in the given list of words-

Arrive	lamb	carry	bat	learn
ride	write	Take	song	bring
like	lick	stay	carrot	see
Pale	peel	chair	cheer	flower
tree	Cut	nut	attack	heart
hear	sing	touch	torch	Sea

Practice 5

Complete the sentences using the verbs given in the box below-

went	drew	sent	play	announced
bloomed	jumped	bought	travelled	saw

A] I ……………..cricket every day.

B] Ajay ………………a message to his friend.

C] He ………..to canteen after the class.

D] The painter ……………. a beautiful painting.

E] We ………….. by train in May.

F] The flowers ……………….. in the garden.

G] The Head master ……………………….a holiday.

H] The children…………………..the bear.

I] A monkey ……………..from the tree.

J] He…………….. a ticket.

2.5 Adverb

Sonu came to school **late today**. Her sister Tina got up **early** but he remained in bed till 8 o'clock. He had played cricket **yesterday** with his friends .He was **very** tired. So her mother allowed her to sleep **more**. Tina went upstairs to bring a chart paper. While coming back she decided to call her friend from the roof of the house. On the roof when she looked **up** she found clouds in the sky. The birds were also **there**. She told her mother that she had seen clouds above the house. Her mother said that clouds would go .She prepared her for school **hurriedly.**

Definition – Adverb is a word which modifies the meanings of verbs, adjectives, prepositions, conjunctions, and other adverbs.

Adverbial words usually end in -*ly*. For example, *properly* in the clause *work properly is* an adverb because it modifies the verb 'work'. But there are many adverbs that do not end in -*ly*. For example, *fast in* the clause *run fast* is an adverb because it modifies the verb *run*.

Though we often speak of adverbs as single words, phrases and clauses can also function as adverbs. For example, in the sentence, "She plays with her left hand," *with his left hand* is an adverbial phrase because it modifies the verb *plays*. And in the sentence, "They sit in the drawing room after finishing kitchen work," *after finishing kitchen work* is an adverbial clause because it modifies the verb *sit*.

Kinds of Adverb

Adverb of Manner:
She entered slowly and sat quietly.

Adverb of Place
John has lived on the sea beach all her life.

She still works <u>there</u> now.

Adverbs of Frequency:
She takes the car to the market <u>every day</u>.
They <u>seldom</u> go there together.

Adverbs of Time:
They try to get back <u>till evening.</u>
It's starting to get cold <u>now</u>.
She finished her homework <u>first</u>.
Deepa left <u>soon</u>.

Adverbs of Purpose:
Harriet drives her car carefully <u>to avoid hitting the walls</u>.
He practices everyday <u>to get the top rank.</u>

Adverb modifies a verb/adjective/adverb/preposition or conjunction-

Examples-

- She slowly closed the book.
In the sentence above, the adverb 'slowly' **modifies the verb** 'closed'.
- The students are studying in properly lit rooms.
In this sentence, the adverb *properly* **modifies the adjective** *lit*:
- She dances really nicely.
Here, the adverb really **modifies the adverb** nicely. (which modifies the verb *dances*)
- The car passed directly through the market.
Here, *directly* **modifies the preposition** *through.*
- Right when I finished my song, everyone started clapping.
Here, the adverb right **modifies the conjunction** *when.*

Formation of adverbs

1. From most adjectives

Most adjectives can be made adverbs by adding a -*ly* to the end—for example, *proper* becomes *properly, quick* becomes *quickly,* and *light* becomes *lightly.*

Adjective	Adverb
nice	nicely
proper	properly
active	actively
beautiful	beautifully
careful	carefully
quick	quickly
slow	slowly

2. From -*ic* adjectives

Adjectives ending in -*ic* are made adverbs by adding -*ally*. For example, *heroic* becomes *heroically, basic* becomes *basically,* and *poetic becomes poetically.*

Adjective	Adverb
economic	economically
fantastic	fantastically
romantic	romantically
sarcastic	sarcastically
tragic	tragically
magic	magically
basic	basically
majestic	majestically
dramatic	dramatically

3. From adjectives ending in -*le*

To make an adverb from an adjective that ends a consonant followed by *-le*, drop the *e* and add *y*. For example, *ample* becomes *amply,* and *gentle* becomes *gently.*

Adjective	Adverb
gentle	gently
horrible	horribly
humble	humbly
terrible	terribly
probable	probably

4. From adjectives ending in *-y*

To make an adverb from an adjective ending in *-y* (but not *-ly*) drop the *y* and add *-ily*—for example *happy* becomes *happily*, *angry* becomes *angrily.*

There are a few -ly adjectives that also function as adverbs. A few of the most common ones are *daily, early, weekly, monthly, hourly, stately, timely, nightly,* and *yearly.*

Adjective	Adverb
happy	happily
ready	readily
angry	angrily
easy	easily
lucky	luckily

Flat adverbs

Some adverbs don't change from their adjectival forms. These are known as flat adverbs. Some of the most common ones are

close, deep, fast, quick, and right.

Some of these have corresponding -*ly* adverbs with which they are interchangeable—for example, *come quick* and *come quickly* mean the same thing.

Proper order of adverbs-

When there are many adverbs in a sentence, they should follow a proper order as shown in the example given below-

Manner   *Place*   <u>**Frequency**</u>   Time   *Purpose*

Radha dances   gracefully   *in the hall* <u>every Sunday</u> in the evening *to perform better.*

He goes curiously *into library* <u>every morning</u> before breakfast *to read a magazine.*

Teena sits lazily *in her classroom* <u>every day</u> during class time *to attend the lecture.*

Uses of Adverbs-

1. Use of adverb with intransitive verbs-

Jumped happily, went hurriedly, came slowly.

2. Use of adverb with transitive verb having object-

He was eating food hurriedly.
She was singing songs happily.
They are taking medicines cautiously.

3. Use of adverb with adjective, preposition, adverb and conjunction –Adverb is placed before adjective, preposition, adverb and conjunction-

Extremely sorry, Very happy, highly surprised **[with adjective]**
Probably inside the room, possibly in the meeting **[with preposition]**

More loudly, how soon, very clearly, almost completely **[with adverb]**
They visited the city **early** because they had to buy wedding items**.**
[with conjunction]

4. Adverb of number (always, never, often, seldom, rarely,) are used before verb.

We **often** visited that park.
He **seldom** told his problem to us.
She **never** speaks loudly.
People **rarely** accept their mistakes.

Practice 1
Fill in the blanks with suitable adverbs.
1. He is ………….late.
2. You should work ………. to pass the examination.
3. Come ………….. . I want to show you something.
4. ………………….. get up early.
5. He was …………..injured.
6. They danced on the stage……………… .
7. He went …………as he had to catch the train.

Practice 2
Fill in the blanks with these words

never always very mostly usually often sometimes rarely

a] You should …………..brush your teeth before going to bed.
b] He …………goes to the dentist.
c] I ……….hire a taxi. I prefer to walk.
d]…………there is heavy traffic in the city roads.
e] They…………spend their summer in a hill station.
f] …………..he comes to my home to take a stapler from my brother.
g] I …………….visit that shop to eat an ice cream.
Answers:
Practice 1: 1.very 2.hard 3.quickly /here 4. Always 5.badly
6.gracefully /nicely 7. hurriedly

Practice 2: a. always b. rarely c. never d. mostly e. often f. Sometimes g. usually

2.6 Preposition

Let us begin with a story.

Two children were sitting **between** guava and mango trees. Some stones were lying **under** the trees. The children could see their shadows in the ground **below.** The trains passed **through** the tunnel .The trees **beside** the track were green. The passengers were watching **out from** the windows of the train coaches. One of the children threw a stone **at** the mango tree. It hit a mango **of** a lower branch. The mango fell **down** .The mango was lying **on** the ground. The child picked the mango **in** his hand. The other boy too threw a stone **at** a bunch **of** mangoes **of** a higher branch. Some of the mangoes fell **between** the trees. It was six o'clock **of** the evening .The sun was going **down**. The children collected the mangoes **in** a bag and moved **towards** their homes. They were going **away from** the railway bridge. One **of** them tried to count the mangoes **by** entering his hand **into** the bag. He brought a mango **out of** the bag and cut it **with** a knife. Then he gave a part of it **to** the other boy.

The bold written words in the above story are prepositions.

Prepositions are words which are kept before a noun to tell its position, place or time.

A Preposition denotes the position that one person or thing occupies in relation to the other.

Prepositions of time are used before the time indicating word.

It is pre (before) because it is put before the noun or noun equivalent which is its object.

Example: The book is on the table.

On in the above sentence is a preposition .It shows the relation of the book to the table.

The rules for some of the most frequently used prepositions in English are as given below:

Prepositions – Time

On   Day of the week- on Monday, on Tuesday, on holiday

In   Months-in August, in June
            Seasons- in winter, in summer
            Part of a day - the morning/ the evening /the afternoon,
            Year- in 2016, in 2020
            A period- in an hour/in a week/in a fortnight

At   For night, weekend, clock time – at night/ at the weekend/ at 7 o'clock

Since   From a certain point of time – since 2014
For   Over a certain period of time- for 2 years /for 6 months/for 3 days

Ago   A certain time in the past – 11 years ago

Before   Earlier than a certain point of time – before 2014

To   Telling the time- Ten to Nine (8:50)

Past   To tell clock time after any hour- five past seven

To/till/until Marking the beginning and end of a period- from Wednesday   to /till Tuesday.

By   In the sense of 'at the latest'/up to a certain time - I will be back by 6 o'clock.

Preposition –Place (Position and direction)

Preposition	Usage	Example
In	• room, building, street, town, country • Book, paper etc. • car, bus • picture, world	• She is in the kitchen. He works in Delhi • in the book • in the car, in a bus • in the picture, in the world
At	• meaning *next to, by an object* • for *table* • for events • place where you are to do something typical (watch a film, study, work)	• I knocked at the door. She waited at the station • at the table • He must be at the post office, • at the party • at the cinema, at school, at work
On	• attached • for a place with a river • being on a surface • for a certain side (left, right) • for a floor in a house • for public transport • for *television,*	• the picture on the wall • London lies on the Thames. • on the table • on the left • on the first floor • on the bus, on a plane • on TV, on the

	radio	radio

By, Next to, Beside	left or right of somebody or something	Rohan is sitting by / next to / beside the car.
Under	on the ground, lower than (or covered by) something else	the bag is under the table
Below	lower than something else but above ground	the fish are below the surface
Over	<ul><li>covered by something else</li><li>meaning *more than*</li><li>getting to the other side (also *across*)</li><li>overcoming an obstacle</li></ul>	<ul><li>put a jacket over your shirt</li><li>over 18 years of age</li><li>walk over the bridge</li><li>climb over the wall</li></ul>
Above	higher than something else, but not directly over it	a path above the lake
Across	<ul><li>getting to the other side (also *over*)</li><li>getting to the other side</li></ul>	<ul><li>walk across the bridge</li><li>swim across the lake</li></ul>
Through	<ul><li>something with limits on top, bottom and the sides</li></ul>	<ul><li>drive through the tunnel</li></ul>

To	• movement to person or building • movement to a place or country • for *bed*	• We shall go to the Restaurant this weekend. • go to Chennai / Sea shore • go to bed
Into	• enter a room / a building	• go into the kitchen / the house
Towards	• movement in the direction of something (but not directly to it)	• Go 5 steps towards the house.
Onto	• movement to the top of something	• jump onto the table
From	• in the sense of *where from*	• He plucked a flower from the garden.

Some other important prepositions

From	• who gave it	• This toy is a present from

		Geeta.
Of	<ul><li>who/what does it belong to</li><li>what does it show</li></ul>	<ul><li>He showed me a page of the book.</li><li>The cover of the book had a picture of a palace.</li></ul>

By	<ul><li>who made it</li></ul>	<ul><li>I have just finished reading a book by R.K.Narayan.</li></ul>
On	<ul><li>walking or riding on horseback</li><li>entering a public transport vehicle</li></ul>	<ul><li>He went to the polling both on foot/on horseback.</li><li>Get on the bus.</li></ul>
In	<ul><li>entering a car / Taxi</li></ul>	<ul><li>Get in the car soon.</li></ul>
Off	<ul><li>leaving a public transport vehicle</li></ul>	<ul><li>Get off the train. It is about to move.</li></ul>
Out of	<ul><li>leaving a car / Taxi</li></ul>	<ul><li>See the meter reading before you get out of the taxi.</li></ul>
By	<ul><li>rise or fall of something</li></ul>	<ul><li>Prices have risen by 10 percent.</li></ul>

	• travelling (other than walking or horse riding)	• He reached the office by car. • You may go by bus.
At	• for *age*	• She learned Telugu at 45.
About	• for topics, meaning *what about*	• We were talking about you.

Practice 1: Prepositions -Place

Complete the exercise with the correct prepositions.

1. I got this toy car ………….my uncle.
2. This toy car was packed……..my cousin, who is 16 years old.
3. ……this toy car you can see a headlight.
4. This is a model ……. a car.
5. Look ……….this car. Isn't it wonderful?

Answers: 1. From 2. by 3.In 4.of 5.at

Practice 2: Prepositions - Time

Fill in the correct prepositions.

1. I play cricket …….Sunday.
2. My sister's birthday is ……. 9th of July.
3. Your birthday is …….September.
4. We are going to see the Taj……..the weekend.
5. …………1984, a great riot took place in Delhi.
6. I don't like to walk alone……….night..
7. What do you do ………the afternoon?
8. My friend has been living in New York ………three years.
9. She has been waiting for you …………five o'clock.
10. You have to finish this essay………Friday.

Answers (Practice2) _1.on 2.on 3.in, 4.in, 5.in 6.at 7.in 8.for 9.since 10.by

Note- Generally a preposition is used before a noun or a pronoun, but there are some circumstances in which this does not happen, either the complement has to take first position in the clause, or because it is absent.

Wh- question:
What were you looking at?
What are you looking for?
Relative clause:
This is the book that we were looking for.
The old house which I was telling you about is empty.
Wh-Clauses-
What I am convinced of is that the world's population will grow to an unforeseen extent.
Exclamations:
What a mess he's got into!
Passive:
She was sought after by all the leading impresarios of the day.
Infinitive Clauses:
He is impossible to work with.

Prepositions are of two kinds-:

Simple prepositions:	Compound prepositions:
At, in ,on, by, with, of ,off, for, from, to, out, over, under, since, through, up, down, after, Round ,till, against	Into, upon, within, without, beneath, Underneath, between, behind, outside, above, Across ,about, beside

USE OF SOME IMPORTANT PREPOSITIONS

Among, between

- **Among** is used for more than two persons or things
- **Between** is used only for two.

Examples:

1. Distribute these sweets among the poor students of the class.
2. She works among the poor.
3. Distribute these books between Ram and Shyam.
4. I lost my book somewhere between the car and the house.

Among, in

- **Among** is used before collective plural nouns
- **In** is used before collective singular nouns.
  Examples:
  1. Found him standing among the crowd.
  2. I saw him in the crowd.

Beside, Besides

- **Beside** means *by the side of*
- **Besides** means *in addition to*

Examples:

1. The daughter was sitting beside her mother.
2. Besides his relatives, he invited his friends also.

In, within (in relation to time),

- **'In'** means at the expiry of a period of time in future.
- **'Within'** means before the expiry of a period of time in any tense.

Examples-

1. She will return in a week.
2. I shall finish my work within a week.

On, Upon

- 'On' is used for things at rest,
- 'Upon' is used for things in motion or things about to happen.

Examples-

1. He is sitting on the floor.
2. The book is on the table.
3. The dog sprang upon the table. (Motion)
4. Diwali is upon us again. (About to happen)

By, With

- 'By' denotes the agent or doer;
- 'With' denotes the instrument with which anything is done.

Example:1. Ravana was killed by Rama with an arrow.
2. The bird was killed by the hunter with an arrow.
3. He beat the dog with an stick.

By is used in future tense to express the time limit (not later than).

Example-

I shall reach there by five o'clock.

With also means the following –

1. in the company or presence of-
I came to Delhi with a friend.
2. Agreement or support-
Are you with us on this issue?
3. Reason-
She trembled with fear.

4. Opposition-

I had an argument with my landlord.

After, in (in relation to time)

- 'After' means at the end of a period of time in the past;
- 'In' means at the end of a period of time in future.

Example-

1. He returned the book after a week.
2. I shall return your book in a week.

For, from, since-

- **For** is used before a noun denoting a period of time with all tenses.
- **From** is used before a noun or phrase denoting a point of time; it is used in all the tenses.
- **Since** is used before a noun or phrase denoting some point of time and is always preceded by a verb in the perfect continuous tense or third form of the verb.

From is generally followed by till or to.

Examples-

1. We have been playing cards for two hours.
2. My elder brother has been ill for four days.
3. She has lived in Mumbai for four years.
4. We play from 5 p.m. to 6p.m. every day.
5. Will your school remain closed from tomorrow till 25th of March.
6. She stayed with her uncle from the 15th of March to the 15th of May.
7. I have been reading this book since morning.
8. My father has been teaching in this school since morning.
9. He has not heard from his uncle since last Monday.

Over, Above-

- 'Over' is used in the following four senses-

1. In the sense of above-
   > At noon the sun is over our heads.
   > There was a lamp over the table.
2. In the sense of beyond-
   > I cannot get over my disappointment.
3. In the sense of superiority-
   > God over all blesses for ever more.
4. In the sense of conclusion-
   > It is all over with me.

- **Above** is used in the following sense-

1. In the sense of higher then-
   > We flew above the clouds.
2. In the sense of more than-
   > Applicants must be above the age of 18.
3. In the sense of greater importance or quality-
   > A soldier values honor above life.
4. In the sense of too honorable or too important to engage in bad qualities-
   > He is above suspicion.

At, towards-

- **At** denotes the idea of aim
- **Towards** denotes the idea of destination/ direction.

Examples-

1. He threw the stone at the cat.
2. Aim the ball at the hole.
3. He went towards the house.
4. He came running towards me.

At, In, On

At is used as follows-

- **At** is used with small towns and villages; as

  He was born at Sonepat.
  He lives at Ramgarh.

- **At** is used before a noun denoting a definite point of time ;as

  He will start at six o'clock in the morning.
  He called on me at 9 p.m. yesterday.

- **'In'** is used as follows:

(a)**In** is used with the names of big cities, provinces and countries, as

  1. His father lives in England.
  2. I live at Panipat in Haryana.
  3. His younger brother lives in Kolkata.

(b)**In** is used before the names of months and years, as

  His elder sister was born in 1972 in the month May.
  He will go to Patna in April.

- **On** is used with dates and names of days, as,

  1. I joined college on 26th April.
  2. He will leave for Chandigarh on Wednesday next.
  3. He will come on Monday.

Note-

- **'At'** can be used before a big city when one stays there for a short time en route to some other place as ,

  While going to Delhi, he will stay at Poona for three days.

- **'At'** is used in the following phrases-

  At night, at midnight, at noon, at day-break, at sunset, at sunrise, at home, at the station, at work, at play

- **'In'** is also used in the following phrases –

In the morning, in the evening, in the afternoon, in winter, in summer

'**In**' also denotes a place inside anything, as,

He travelled in a crowded bus.
Put it in a box.

Below, beneath

- **Below** means of lower level in position, dignity and expectation, etc
- **Beneath** means under

Examples

1. A sergeant in the police force is below an inspector.
2. It is below my dignity to talk to her.
3. They found gold coins beneath a pile of leaves.

In, into, to

- '**In**' expresses rest or motion inside anything.
- '**Into**' expresses motion towards the inside of anything or change from one medium to another.
- '**To**' denotes motion from one place to another.

Examples-

1. Sita is in bed.
2. The boys are in the room.
3. He poured tea into a cup.
4. Every morning he goes to the temple.
5. They are going to France.

'**To**' is also used in the following senses:
- towards a condition, state of quality:

She tore the letter to pieces.
- as for as:

The garden extends to the river bank.
* a moment in time or time before an exact hour:
The party continued from morning to night.

Till, By, Of, Off

* 'Till' means up to or not earlier than.
* 'By' means not later than.
* 'Of' shows cause, source, separation, quality, contents, possession, apposition, point of reference, space in time, etc.
* 'Off' shows separation at a near distance, and detached condition.

Examples-

1. I shall work till 5 a.m.
2. By this time tomorrow, I will have finished my job.
3. Madhu died of Cancer.(cause)
4. The nib of the pen is made of gold.(source)
5. He presented me a bottle of whiskey.(contents)
6. He was deprived of luxury and comfort .(separation)
7. Our principal is a man of principle.(quality)
8. He lived in the house of his friend.(possession)
9. Mohan, the son of Mr.Ramlal, got married.
10. We are talking about the school 5 miles east of Delhi.(point of reference)
11. He came back within an hour of the appointed time.(point of reference)
12. My house is off the road.(separated from the main road by a short distance)
13. The book fell off the table.(detached)

Across, Along, Through

- '**Across**' means from one side to the other side of something, on or to the other side of something.

Example-The ball rolled across the lawn.

The bus came towards them across the bridge.

We use '**over**' rather than '**across**' when we talk about reaching the other side of something, which is higher than it is wide.

Example-He jumped over the wall.

- '**Along**' means from one end towards the other .It also means close to or parallel with.

Examples-

They walked along the footpath.
I saw him walking along the road.
They are planning to go for a picnic along the river bank.

- **Through** refers to movement in a three dimensional space, with things all around. It often suggests movement from one side or end of space to the other.

Examples: He pushed his way through the crowd of people to get to her.

She walked through the forest to get to her friend's house.

Verbs followed by prepositions

agree about	They agreed about changing the site.
argue about	The teachers argued about setting the timetable.
care about	Who cares about increasing pollution?
complain about	She complains about hair fall.

forget about	Raj forgets about my birthday gift.
talk about	Susan talks about getting employed.
think about	They are thinking about calling us.
worry about	I am worried about getting late.
dream about	She dreams about being famous.
decide against	She decided against taking loan.
warn against	The Government warned against hiding the income.

look after	Mary will look after boiling the milk.
delight at	I was delighted at seeing you again.
excel at	She excels at singing songs.
laugh at	We laughed at dressing in a funny way.
rejoice at	He rejoiced at winning the match.
apologize for	I apologized for getting late.
blame for	I was blamed for missing the goal.
care for	I don't care for buying tickets.
stand for	They won't stand for playing loud music.

keep from	I tried to keep from seeing her.
suffer from	He suffers from Malaria.
refrain from	The people refrained from smoking.
stop somebody from	The constable stopped them from entering in the building.
believe in	He believes in being regular in duties.
deal in	The Sharmas deal in selling mangoes.
engage in	Hari engages in starting up new websites.
give in/into	He won't give into his requests.
interested in	He is interested in playing hockey.
participate in	He will participate in cluster level games.
result in	Carelessness can result in an failure.
specialize in	He will specialize in heart transplantation.
succeed in	She succeeded in getting admission.
accuse of	Raj was accused of hiding the facts.
approve of	The judge didn't approve of his behavior.

dream of	He dreams of becoming a scientist.

in charge of	I am in charge of sending the invitations.
take care of	Rohit took care of getting correct tickets.
think of	They thought of a new plan to attract customers.
call off	The manager called off the meeting.
put off	He put off attending coaching classes.
think over	I am thinking over joining a coaching class.
talk over	They talked over opening a shop.
agree on	Raj agreed on teaching in a school.
concentrate on	She concentrates on joining a course of fashion designing.
congratulate on	They congratulated us on our success.
continue on	He continued on playing all day.
Depend on	She depends on getting education loan.
go on	I shall go on making effort to pass that exam.
insist on	She insists on joining an orchestra.
intend on	He intends on opening a school.
keep on	They keep on requesting.
plan on	She plans on reducing weight.
rely on	You may rely on our advices.
adjust to	They adjusted to living in the Canada
agree to	We agreed to going by train.
devote to	He is devoted to working.
used to	We are used to listening loud noise of cars.
look forward	We look forward to seeing him.
object to	He objects to eating food in hotels.

agree with	He agrees with reading news daily.
charge with	She was charged with murder.
mess with	We don't want to mess with hiring a taxi.
trust with	You wouldn't trust him with doing it alone.

Nouns followed by prepositions

access to	All the classrooms have access to the internet.
advantage of	The thief too advantage of electricity failure to enter the house.
advantage over	His height gave him an advantage over others.

admiration for	We have great admiration for him as an actor.

attack on	It was a fetal attack on terrorists.
attitude to/towards	Your attitude towards him is not good.
authority on	He is an authority on Mathematics.
association with something	He became famous through his association with a leader.
commend on	He was commended on his success in installing the system.
comparison with	His comparison with Pele was not right.
connection between	There is no connection between this crime and his presence there.
contrast with	Your behavior contrasts with your words.
credit for	The credit for this success goes to Mr.Sharma.
cruelty towards	Cruelty towards animals is a criminal offence.
characteristic of	Innocence and honesty are the characteristics of saints.
decrease in	There is a constant decrease in crime.
delay in	There should be no delay in distribution of papers.
desire for	He had a great desire for collecting a lot of wealth.
difference between/of	There is a great difference between the two books.
difficulty in/with	He feels difficulty in lifting the bucket due to her arm injury.
disadvantage of	The disadvantage of over population is felt everywhere.
effect on	The accident had a great effect on his efficiency.
exception to	There was an exception to this rule.
expert on/at/in	He is a great expert in this field.
experience in	I have five years experience in editing news articles.
hope for	Let us hope for the best.
increase in	There was a great increase in crime rate.
influence on	The influence of smoking on lungs can be examined.
information about	Do you have any information about that case?

intention of	I had no intention of travelling without ticket.
knowledge of	Knowledge of English will help you a lot.
lack of	There was no lack of money.
link with	This channel links Europe with Asia.
matter with	She is upset today. What is the matter with her?
need for	There is an urgent need for experienced salesmen.
notice of	He took no notice of the ditch on the road.
opinion of/about	What is your opinion about this new project?
pleasure in	She takes no pleasure in her job.
preference for	They showed their preference for the swimming pool.
protection against	This policy offers protection against road accidents.
reaction to	What was her reaction to the offer?
recipe for	His plans are a recipe for troubles.
reduction in	There has been some reduction in poverty.
relationship with	He has a close relationship with his cousins.
report on	The commission will submit its report on taxes tomorrow.
responsibility for	You are appointed as a manager with responsibility for Online sales.
result of	This success is the result of your hard work.
respect for	She has no respect for his feelings.
rise in	This has been constant rise in the number of unemployed people.
room for	There is no room for laziness in the path of success.
Solution to	In this book you will get solution to most of your problems.
smell of	The smell of rose is sweet.
sympathy for	I have no sympathy for criminals.
tax on	The government has increased tax on cigarettes.
taste of	The taste of this juice is sweet.
threat to	This is a threat to our national integrity.
trouble with	The trouble with the old people is that they don't believe in the new ideas.
use of	There is no use of this inverter.

victim of	He became a victim of old rivalry of the two families.

Adjectives followed by prepositions

accustomed to	I am accustomed to having sleep in the afternoon.
accused of	He was accused of robbery.
acquainted with	I am acquainted with that person.
addicted to	He is addicted to gambling.
annoyed about/with/at	My father was annoyed with me about the untidy room.
allergic to	She is allergic to dust.
amazed at/by	They were amazed by our hospitality.
anxious about	I am anxious about train reservations.
appreciated for	He was appreciated for his sincerity.
ashamed of	You should be ashamed of your behavior.
associated with	I am not associated with any party.
astonished at/by	We were astonished at the news.
aware of	He is very well aware of the facts.
angry with	Don't be angry with me. I am your well wisher.
afraid of	Are you afraid of anything?
attached to	There is no risk attached to this product.
bad at	He is bad at typing.
based on	This news is based on inputs received from correspondences.
beneficial to	This medicine is beneficial to health.
bored with	They very often get bored with sitting continuously.
busy with	I am busy with my assignment.
capable of	Are you capable of controlling the crowd?
careful with/about/of	You must be careful of the traffic while driving a bike. Be careful with my camera.
certain about	Was she certain about her statement?
characteristic of	Keen observation is a key characteristic of a scientist.
clever at	He is clever at choosing gift for himself.
connected with	This job is connected with keeping files

	properly.
conscious of	He is conscious of his duties.
content with	Are you content with your position in the class?
crazy about	He is crazy about her.
crowded with	The bus was crowded with passengers.
curious about	I am curious about his qualifications.

Practice3

Fill in the blanks with correct preposition-

1. He is devoid……..sense.(from/of/in)
2. The teacher was standing………..the pupils.(between/among)
3. This letter is written ………..my friend.(with/by/from)
4.He laughed ………..us.(on/at/of)
5.I took my younger brother ………..me to school.(from/with/at/to)
6.He goes …..bus.(in/by/with)
7. When can I get a train ……..Jaipur? (to/with/for)
8.He paid four hundred rupees ……..that shirt.(for/to/with)
9.The girl was playing………….a doll.(by/with/at)
10. He died…………cholera.(at/of/with)
Answers: 1. of 2.among 3.by 4. at 5. with 6.by 7.for 8.for 9.with10.of

Practice 4

Fill in the blanks with correct preposition-
1. We had to write it………..ink.
2. They had to wait ………..the bus stop for two hours.
3 I knocked ……………door but no one answered.
4. I go …………..school by bus.

5. My friend reaches school ....foot.

6. I received this watch on the fifth.............March.

7. I haven't seen you ....three days.

8. Father complained ....the postman.

9. He sold his house ....a small sum.

10.Cut it ....a knife.

Answer- 1.in 2.at 3.at 4.to 5.on 6. of 7.for 8.against 9 . for 10. with

Practice5

Fill in the blanks with correct preposition-

1. Smoking is injurious ....health.

2. He was afraid..........punishment.

3. Hard work is key..........success.

4. His thirst ....knowledge took him to great heights.

5. The proofs point ....a different conclusion.

6. He acted according ....my plan.

7. You are disqualified ....practicing as a lawyer.

8. It is the result ....your hard work.

9. I have no prejudice ....you.

10. She met me ....my way to the station.

Answer: 1.to 2.of 3.to 4.for 5.to 6.to7. from 8.of 9.against 10.on

Practice 6

Fill in the blanks with suitable prepositions-

(i) She is junior..........me.

(ii) She shook him .... the hand.

(iii)I was appointed ....the post of a clerk.

(iv)Mrs.Gupta is eager ....promotion.

(v)He is good..........Mathematics.

(vi)We do not believe ....such news.

(vii)They were overjoyed...........the prospect of meeting the cricketer.

(viii) You must be faithful…………your friend.
(ix)Salt is not…………stock.
(x) You must beware ……….stray dogs.
Answers: i)to ii)by iii)to iv)for v)at vi)in vii) at viii)to ix)out of x)of

Practice 7

Fill in the blanks with suitable prepositions-

(i)She died ………………………….Cholera.
(ii) The sports week will start….. 27th July.
(iii) He was dressed …………………white.
(iv) My cousin lives…………..…….Chennai.
(v) They will visit the school……Tuesday.
(vi) You can depend ………………his advice.
(vii) It will stop the blood ……….flowing.
(viii) I stayed …………home that day.
(ix) Mr.Rohit Sharma has been appointed ……the of PGT(Physics)
(x) Husband and wife must be faithful …………each other.
Answers- i)of ii)from iii)in iv)in v)on vi)on vii)from viii)at ix)to x)to

Practice 8

Fill in the blanks with suitable prepositions:
a) You must be indebted ……….him………his kindness.
b) She killed the mouse …………a poker.
c) Deepak burst……….tears.
d) She has been suffering from fever………….last night.
e) One must stick …………his/her decision.
f) You should not interfere …………his matters.
g) They invited me…………….lunch.
h) We are looking forward…………your positive reply.
i) We abstain ……….wine.
j) Rajiv insisted ……..taking tea.

Answer-a)to, for b)with c)into d)since e)to f)in g)to h) to i)from j)on
Practice 9

1.Suger sells..........Rs.30/- a kilo.

2.They do not agree ....what we believe.

3. I have been waiting .... your letter.

4.The boys listened .... the music.

5.Don't laugh ....the poor begger.

6. You will see there a boy ....blue eyes.

7. This shirt is made ....cotton.

8. Rajkumar was married ....a journalist.

9. I asked him .... his health.

10. The train will depart ....9.00 p.m.

Answers: 1 at 2 with 3 for 4 to 5 at 6with 7 of 8 to 9 about 10 at

Practice 10.

1.Arun is sure ....his success.

2. No candidate was found fit...........this job.

3. You should not laugh ....the poor people.

4. He bought that pen..........Rs.5.

5. The leader went ....door........door.

6. This apple juice is good ....you.

7. The property was divided ....five sons.

8. We should thank him ....his advice.

9. Are you sure............his age?

10. He is kind ....all his students.

Answers:1.of 2.for 3.at 4.for 5.from,to 6.for 7 between 8. for 9.about 10.to

Practice 11

1. I am ashamed ......your conduct.

2. He is fond ....music.

3. She is clever.........mathematics.

4. You should be faithful ....your friends.

5. Do you believe ……………this news?

6. Did he agree ………………your proposal?

7. The people were complaining ………their hardships.

8. Are you in search …………a good house?

9. Rajeev comes ………………a business family.

10. This watch belongs …..my father.

11. Arun is married…….Deepa.

12. Is this book useful …………students ?

13. They were going……..Bhopal.

14. Ravi went to Agra….train.

15. My neighbour has no control …….his children.

16. This diary deals…………….life in mountains.

17. Let us hope………….a better season.

18.She stopped her……….going there.

19. Has she borrowed any money……..you?

20.Water is compulsory ………life on Earth.

Answers:1. of 2.of 3.at 4.to 5.in 6.with 7.about 8.of 9.of 10.to

11.to 12.for 13.to 14.by 15.over 16.with17.for18.from 19.from 20.for

2.7 Conjunctions

Let us read this story first:

I waited for my friend whole afternoon **but** he did not turn up. I could not guess what may be the reason. **Though** I missed him very much I did not call her on phone. **Before** I could think of calling him he himself called me. He told me that he would come **after** his father's return from the bank. **As soon as** he told me this I changed my plan of going to cinema with him. I too remembered **that** I had to go to bank **for** taking my ATM card from there. I hurried towards the bank **as** only 30 minutes were left in bank's closing time. **Not only** the bank was away from my house **but** the fact that next day was a holiday **also**

117

made me walk quickly. Only five minutes were left for its closing **when** I reached the bank. The clerk took my sign in a register **and** handed me over an envelope containing ATM card.

While coming back from bank I remembered that my friend has told me that he would come to my home. I did not want to disappoint him **therefore** I started walking at fast pace. Fortunately he had just arrived at my home **and** was asking about me. He saw me **and** asked me about the envelope in my hand. I wanted to know **if** he was still willing to go to the cinema hall. I suggested that **either** we should go to cinema immediately **or** spend time playing chess at home. He agreed to my plan **and** preferred to play chess. **Though** I had been thinking about my new ATM Card, I could concentrate on the game. We were busy in playing chess **so** my mother did not ask any question to my friend about his family. She brought some biscuits and tea for us .We continued playing till six p.m.

The bold words in the story are called conjunctions.

Conjunctions are also called connectors. Conjunctive words link two similar elements in a sentence.

Example-
      John and William **are** cousins.
      Two **and** two make four.
      He walked fast **but** missed the bus.
      Work hard **or** you will fail.
      He did not come, **nor** did he send any message.
      He worked hard **but** failed.
      Time flies fast, **yet** it sometimes appears to move slowly.
      You have achieved an excellence, **so** you shall not go unrewarded.

Different kinds of conjunctions join different kinds of grammatical structures.

The following are the kinds of conjunctions:

1. Coordinating conjunctions
2. Subordinating conjunctions
3. Correlating conjunctions
4. Conjunctive Adverbs

1. Coordinating Conjunctions

Coordinating Conjunctions are of four kinds-

1. Cumulative or copulative –**and**
2. Adversative –**but, still, only**
3. Disjunctive or alternative-**or, nor, neither, else**
4. Illative-**for**

In short they can be remembered by term- FANBOYS

FOR, AND, NOR, BUT, OR, YET, SO

Coordinating conjunctions join <u>equals</u> to one another:

Words to words,
Phrases to phrases,
Clauses to clauses

Example:

Word to word: Most of the kids like <u>chocolate</u> **and** <u>milk</u>.
Phrase to phrase: The book is hidden <u>in the box</u> **or** <u>under the bag</u>.
Clause to clause: <u>What you say</u> **and** <u>what you write</u> are two different things.

Coordinating conjunctions go <u>in between</u> items joined, not at the beginning or end.

Example:

>I like coffee, but I don't like tea.
>I want three cups of tea and two cups of coffee.
>He went to office and started his work.
>You can have an apple or an orange.
>They will win or they will lose.
>This shirt is not for Rahul, but Ritesh.
>He was very poor yet very happy.
>The actor was rather young, yet his role was good.

<u>Punctuation with coordinating conjunctions:</u>

When a coordinating conjunction joins **two** words, phrases, or subordinate clauses, no comma should be placed before the conjunction.

Example:

Words:	cookies and milk
Phrase:	in the box or under the bag.
Subordinate clauses:	What you say and what you write

A coordinating conjunction joining **three or more** words, phrases, or subordinate clauses creates a series and requires commas between the elements.

Example-

Words:	peanuts, chocolate, and milk
Phrases:	in the mountains, at the sea shore, or by the lakeside
Subordinate clauses:	what you think, what you write, and what you do.

A coordinating conjunction joining **two independent clauses** creates a compound sentence and requires a comma before the coordinating conjunction.

Example-

> Thomas ate all the peanuts, so John ate the biscuits.
> I don't care for the sea shore, but I enjoy a good vacation in the mountains.
> He saw the danger, but pressed on.
> Do as I suggested, or you will regret it.
> Keep quiet, or you will be seen.

2. Correlative conjunctions

Either ...or	Both...and
Neither ...nor	not only...but also

These pairs of conjunctions require equal (parallel) structures after each one.

Faulty-	Dinesh not only wants money but also respect.
Correct-	Dinesh wants not only money but also respect.
Correct-	Dinesh not only wants money but also wants respect.

More examples:

Either come on time **or** forget about the reservation.
Either rice **or** wheat is required.
Either take it **or** leave it.
Either it is right, **or** it is wrong.

Not only is he foolish, **but also** rude.
I can **not only** hear him, **but also** see him.
He was **not only** fined **but also** expelled.

Both Ram **and** his brother attend coaching class.

Both the president **and** the prime minister were there.
He can speak **both** Hindi **and** English.

Neither Deepak **nor** Dileep passed the exam.
Neither he **nor** his brother arrived here.
I am **neither** angry **nor** happy.

The more you earn **the more** you spend.
The more he invested **the more** he lost.
The more he achieved **the more** he became humble.

I shall go there **whether** I am allowed to **or not.**
You are capable **whether** you accept it **or not.**

Paired correlative conjunctions:

Of time	no sooner...than
	Hardly ...when
	scarcely ...when
	barely...when

No sooner ....than

If the second event occurs immediately after the first, we can express that idea using the structure 'no sooner than'. 'No sooner' introduced the event that occurred first.

No sooner had I arrived at the station **than** the train came. (= I came first)
No sooner had we heard the sound **than** we rushed to the spot.
No sooner had I closed my eyes **than** I fell asleep.

Hardly and scarcely-

It is possible to express the same idea using hardly /scarcely…when.

Hardly had I reached the station **when** the train came.
Scarcely had I reached the station **when** the train arrived.
Hardly had the plane taken off, **than** the pilot reported some trouble.

As soon as-

As soon as I arrived at the station, the train came.
As soon as the peon rang the bell the students ran out of the class.
She will handle it **as soon as** she comes here.

3. CONJUNCTIVE ADVERBS

These conjunctions join independent clauses together.

The following are frequently used conjunctive adverbs:

after all	*in addition*	*none the less*
as a result	*incidentally*	*next*
also	*in fact*	*on the contrary*
besides	*indeed*	*on the other hand*
consequently	*in other words*	*otherwise*
finally	*instead*	*still*
for example	*likewise*	*then*
furthermore	*meanwhile*	*therefore*
hence	*moreover*	*thus*
however	*nevertheless*	*notwithstanding*

Example-

> The tire was flat; therefore, we called a service station.
> It was a hot day; nevertheless, the roofers worked on the
> project all day.

Punctuation: Place a semicolon before the conjunctive adverb and a comma after the conjunctive adverb.

4. Subordinating conjunctions

Subordinating conjunctions combine two or more simple sentences to make a complex sentence. There are a lot of different subordinating conjunctions: normally they link two clauses within a single sentence, so that one clause is subordinated to the other. In other words, the subordinate clause clarifies, expands or explains the meaning of the main clause.

These words are commonly used as subordinating conjunctions

Of time	before ,after, until, ,till, since ,Ere, when, whenever, while, as soon as
Of cause and reason	because, ,since, as, why, given
Or purpose	that, lest, in order to, so that, in order that
Of result and consequences	so…that,such…..that
Of condition	if ,unless, lest
Of contrast	though, although, while
Of comparison	as, than, as…as
Of place	where, wherever, anywhere, everywhere
Of Manner	as, like ,the way

Subordinating conjunctions also join two clauses together, but in doing so; they make one clause dependent (or "subordinate") upon the other.

Example-

It is raining
We have an umbrella.

Both are independent clauses, simple sentences.
Add because to 'it is raining'.
'Because it is raining' - this is no longer an independent clause.
Put the two clauses together-

Because it is raining, we have an umbrella.

Or

We have an umbrella because it is raining.

A subordinating conjunction may appear at a sentence beginning or between two clauses in a sentence.

More Examples-

I am going to Bhopal **because** I have got a new job.
Since it's raining, I am going inside the house.
As she had already taken enough tea, she didn't want any more.
I am locking the window **so that** nobody can peep in.
Although I like him, I wouldn't want to marry him.
After I finished work, I went straight home.
Until they opened a new office, they could not work well.
He asked the driver **whether** he knew the road to the Railway station.
I would not believe him, **whatever** he says.
The man said **that** he worked in a factory.
The chocolate was **so** tasty **that** I bought it for my whole family.

Punctuation Note: When the dependent clause is placed first in a sentence, use a comma between the two clauses. When the independent clause is placed first and the dependent clause second do not separate the two clauses with a comma.

Example:

Because it is raining, we have an umbrella. [First clause is dependent clause]

We have an umbrella because it is raining. [First clause is independent clause]

Practice 1
Combine these sentences:

1a. Mend your ways.

  b. You will have to regret later.

2a. Seeta was scolded.

  b. She was expelled from class.

3a. This is the news.

  b. Rohit sent it.

4a.He can read English.

  b.He cannot speak English.

5a.He was found guilty.

  b.He was sent to jail for five years.

6a.He could not reach early.

  b.His friend reached early.

7a.He worked till late night.

  b.He could not complete the   assignment.

8a.Here is the girl.

  b.You wanted to see.

9a.I was ill.

  b.I could not attend the meeting.

10a.He is poor.

  b.He is happy.

Answers:
1. Mend your ways **otherwise** you will have to regret later. 2.Seeta was **not only** scolded **but also** expelled from class. 3. This is the news **which** Rohit sent. 4. He can read English **but** he cannot speak English.5.He was found guilty **therefore** he was sent to jail for five years. 6. He could not reach **so** early **as** his friend.7. **Though** he worked till late night he could not complete the assignment.8.Here is the girl **whom** you wanted to see. 9. **Since** I was ill, I could not attend the meeting.10.**Though** he is poor, he is happy.

Practice 2
[and, but, or ,so, ,though, till, because Even though]

Combine these pair of sentences into one using suitable conjunction.

1a. He can sell clothes.

  b. He can earn profit.

2a. Work hard.

  b. You will fail.

3a. He stole money.

  b. He was sent to jail.

4a. Keep silent.

  b. Go away.

5a. She wants to buy a shirt.

  b. I want a tie.

6a. You can wait here.

  b. I come back.

7a. He is poor.

  b. He is happy.

8a. He started late form home.

  b. He didn't miss the train.

9a. I like trains .

  b. They move fast.

10a. He is rich.

  b. He lives simple life.

Answers: 1.He can sell clothes **and** earn profit.2.Work hard **or** you will fail.3.He stole money **so** he was sent to jail.4.Keep silent **or** go away.5.She wants to buy a shirt **but** I want a tie.6.You can wait here **till** I come back.6.You can wait here **till** I come back.7.**Though** he is poor he is happy. 8. **Even though** he started late form home he didn't miss the train. 9. I like trains **because** they move fast.10. **Even though** he is rich he lives simple life.

Practice 3

[Who, when, as, what, while, hence, that, which, since]

1a. He was absent.

  b. He was seriously ill.

2a. He reached the station.

  b. The train had gone.

3a. The bell rang.

b.We entered in the class.

4a.I saw the dog.

b.I was going to school.

5a. This was it.

b.What did he tell?

6a I received her call.

b.I was in the train.

7a.He gave his life for motherland.

b.We honour us.

8a. This is the fort.

b. Akbar like this fort most.

9a.They have a watch.

b. The watch is imported.

10a.You are late.

b.You can not appear in examination.

Answers: 1.He was absent **as** he was seriously ill.2.He reached the station **after** the train had gone.3. We entered in the class **when** the bell rang.4.I saw the dog **as** I was going to school.5.This was **what** he told.6.I received her call **while** I was in train.7.He gave his life for motherland **hence** we honour him. 8.This is the fort **that** Akbar liked most.9. They have a watch **which** is imported.10.**Since** you are late you cannot appear in examination.

Practice 4
[How, after, before, than, who, why, because, still, where]

1a. They don't know it.

b. How can one apply for bank clerk's recruitment test?

2a. You came later.

b. The tea was finished.

3a.I had left the office.

b. He came later.

4a.This town is nearer .

b.That town is near.

5a.This is the man.

b. His son got first prize.

6a.Why did he refuse to play?

b.Can you tell me the reason?

7a. This is the shop.

b. The finest suitcases are sold here.

8a. He is poor.

b. He is happy.

9a. He started late form home.

b. He did not miss the train.

10 a. I like trains.

   b. They move fast.

Answers: 1.They do not know **how** to apply for the bank clerk's recruitment test.2. You came **after** the tea was finished.3.I had left the office **before** you came. 4.This town is nearer **than** that town.5.This is the man **who** got the first prize.6.Can you tell me the reason **why** he refused to play.7.This is the shop where the finest suitcases are sold. 8.He is poor still he is happy. 9.He started late form home **still** he did not miss the train.10. I like trains **because** they move fast.

Practice 5

[still, nevertheless, consequently, however, as if, whether, therefore, still , so...as]

1a. He wastes most of his time in talking.

b. He is always late in his work.

2a.He comes to office a little late.

b. All his assignments are complete.

3a. The bags were very heavy.

b. I used the lift to go to the second floor.

4a. He was tired.

b. He continued working.

5a. It appears.

b. The crops will fail.

6a.I do not know.

b. The room is locked.

7a. They cheated in the exam.

b. They were expelled from the examination centre.

8a. He lives far away from school.

b. He reaches in prayer timely.

9a. Deepak ran fast.

 b. His brother ran faster.

10a.You can wait here.

 b.I come back.

Answers: 1.He wastes most of his time in talking **consequently** he is always late in his work. 2.He comes to office a little late **nevertheless** all his assignments are complete.3.The bags were heavy **consequently** I used the lift to go to second floor.4.He was tired **however** he continued working.5.It appears **as if** the crops will fail. 6.I do not know whether the room is locked.7.They cheated in the exam **therefore** they were expelled from the examination centre. 8. He lives far away from school **nevertheless** he reaches in prayer timely. 9. Deepak did not run as fast as his brother. 10.You can wait here **till** I come back.

Practice 6
Combine these pair of sentences using suitable conjunction:
[If, even if, even though, as...as]

1a. She gets a high income.
  b. She would not change her home.
2a. He would not take that bag.
  b. You give the bag to him for free.
3a. I had time.
  b. I would not see that film.
4a. He is rich.
  b. He lives in a simple life.
5a. She washed the shirt many times.
  b. The stain would not go.
6a. The ground was small.
  a. The players played very well.
7a. Work hard.
  b. You will pass the test.
8a. It rains.
  b. I shall not go to market.
9a. You get first division.
  b. You will get award by the principal.
10a. He is selfish.
  b. He is coward.

Answers: 1.**Even if** she gets a high income, she would not change her home.2. He would not take that bag **even if** you give it to him for free. 3. **Even if** I had time I would not see that film. 4. **Even though** he is rich he lives a simple life. 5. **Even though** she washed the shirt many times the stain would not go. 6. **Even though** the ground was small the players played very well. 7. **If** you work hard you will pass the test. 8. **If** it rains I shall not go to market. 9. **If** you get first division you will get award by the Principal. 10. He is **as** selfish **as** coward.

Practice 7
Combine these pair of sentences using suitable conjunctions:
[both...and, unless, therefore , which, whose, not only...but also]

1a. He was tired.
  b. He was sad.

2a. We were happy.
  b. We were excited.

3a. The snacks were good.
  b. The tea was good.
4a. The players were skilled.
  b. The players were agile.
5a. The principal wanted to get high success rate.
  b. He wanted to receive recognition.
6a. You do not work hard.
  a. You will not pass the exam.
7a. You should hire a taxi.
  b. You cannot reach the Railway station in time.
8a. He was guilty.
  b. He was sent to jail.
9a. Raj told me a story.
  b. The story was very interesting.
10a. The girl's mother is a teacher.
   b. The girl was eating lunch with me.

Answers: 1.He was **both** tired **and** sad. 2. We were **both** happy and **excited.**3.**Both** tea **and** snacks were good. 4. The players were **both** skilled **and** agile.5. The principal **not only** wanted to get high success rate **but also** wanted to receive recognition. 6. **Unless** you work hard you will not pass the exam. 7. **Unless** you hire a taxi you cannot reach the station in time. 8. He was found guilty **therefore** he was sent to jail. 9. Raj told me a story **which** was very interesting.10.The girl **whose** mother is a teacher was eating lunch with me.

Practice 8

Combine these pair of sentences using suitable conjunctions:

[as soon as , neither.... nor   either......or   not only........ but also]

1a. She is pretty.
  b. She is intelligent.
2a. He lost his money.
  b. He lost his honour.
3a. I am tired.
  b. I am hungry.
4a. The bell rang.
  b. The students ran out of the classrooms.
5a. He was not playing cricket.

131

b. He wasn't going to market.

6a. He didn't bring a bag.

  b. He didn't bring a suitcase.

7a. She doesn't know Marathi.

  b. She doesn't know Hindi.

8a. The dance wasn't good.

  b. The dinner was not good.

9a. You may take coffee.

  b. You may take tea.

10a. He has fallen ill.

  b. He has missed the train.

Answers:**1.**She is **not only** pretty **but also** intelligent.**2.** He lost **not only** his money **but also** his honour.**3.**I am **both** tired **and** hungry.**4. As soon as** the bell rang the students ran out of the class. **5.**He was **neither** playing cricket **nor** going to market. **6.**He brought **neither** a bag **nor** a suitcase. **7.**She knows **neither** Hindi nor Marathi. **8.Neither** the dinner **nor** the dance was good. **9.**You may take **either** coffee **or** tea. **10.**He has **not only** fallen ill **but also** missed the train.

2.8 Interjection

Let us read these two poems to understand how interjections are used.

1.The stolen Toy- by S.K.Jain

Well! Would you believe it now,

My toy is gone!

So, I asked all friends, "Er, have you seen my toy?"

But they always answered,

"Ah, no. Sorry."

Ah-ha! I'll look over the staircase!

Oh! There's my toy!

Uh, I wonder why it's playing at the staircase, its being...

PLAYFUL!

2. The Key Chain Lost   By: S.K.Jain

Well! Look at that I lost again.

Darn, this bad luck.

I'm a nerd, well yeah.

My family travelled everywhere.

Delhi, Jaipur everywhere yeah!

Baby, gentlemen

Pow! Pee! Pow!

Alleluia! It's over.

Darn it!

Oh, man!

My purse fell down.

And fell from it that lost key chain.

Oh! How happy I am again.

Wow! How easily the chain is gained.

Interjections are words used to express strong or sudden feeling or emotion. They are included in a sentence (usually at the start) to express a sentiment such as surprise, disgust, joy, excitement, or enthusiasm. An interjection is not grammatically related to any other part of the sentence.

Examples of interjections:

> Hey! Get off that window.
> Oh, that is surprise.
> Good! Now we can start our work.
> Hurrah! I have won the game.
> Alas! He is dead.
> Bravo! You did it.
> Wow! I won the lottery!
> Oh, I don't know about that.
> No, you shouldn't have done that.

Some interjections are sounds-

> Phew! I am not trying that again.
> Humph! I knew that last week.
> Mmmm! My compliment to the chef.

Most mild interjections are treated as parenthetical elements and set off from the rest of the sentence with a comma or set of commas. If the interjection is more forceful, however, it is followed with an exclamation mark. Interjections are rarely used in formal or academic writing.

Interjections do not always come at the beginning of a sentence. For example, if you said "So, you don't like spinach too much, huh?" "Huh" would be the interjection on the end of that sentence, designed to convey the emotion or confusion. Interjections can even be found in the middle of a sentence.

List of interjections:

Absolutely,Aha,Ahem,Ahoy,Agreed,Alas,Alright,Alrighty,Alack,Amen,Anytime,Argh,Anyhoo,Anyhow,As if, Atta boy, Atta girl, Awful, Bam, Bah humbug, Behold, Bingo, Blah, Bless you, Boo, Bravo, Cheers, Dang, Drat, Eh, Gee, , Goodness Gracious, Gosh, Ha, Hallelujah, Hey, Hi, Hmm, Huh, Indeed, Mygosh,No,Now,Nah,Oops,Ouch,Phew,Please,Rats,Shoot,Shucks,There,Tut,Uggh,Waa,What,Woah,Woop,Wow,Yay,Yes,Yikes

Kinds of interjections-

1. Interjections for Greeting- These interjections are used to indicate emotion of warmth towards the other person when they meet. Hello! , Hey! , Hi! etc. are such interjections.
Hey! Good to meet you here.
Hello! I am Mary.

2. Interjection for joy-These interjections are used to indicate immediate emotion of happiness on a sudden happy event that occurred. 'Hurrah!', 'Hurray!',and 'Wow!' are such interjections.
Examples-
Hurrah! I got selected in the team.
Wow! I passed the exam.

3. Interjection for approval-These interjections are used to express a strong sense of approval and agreement on something that happened. Bravo! , Brilliant! , Well Done! etc. are such interjections.
Examples-
Well done! You got grade A.
Bravo! He won the match.

4. Interjection for surprise-These interjections are used to express strong sense of surprise on something that happened. Ha!, Hey!, What!, Oh!, Ah !, Eh! Etc. are such interjections.
Example-
What! He failed in the exam!
Ah! I got selected.

5. Interjection for grief or pain-These interjections are used by the speaker when he expresses a strong emotion of grief on something unfortunate that happened. Alas! , Ah! Oh!, Ouch ! etc. are such interjections.
Examples-
Alas! He is dead.
Ouch! I hurt my knee.

3. Sentences

A sentence is a group of words arranged in a specific order which makes complete sense.

A sentence is made of two parts-subject and predicate. Subject of a sentence is a place or thing about which something is stated.

For example – Raj plays cricket.

In the above sentence something is said about Raj so 'Raj' is subject.

Subject may be of one word or of more than one word. For example in the sentence 'The cows of Ram are black.' the subject is 'The cows of Ram'.

Whatever is said about the subject is called its predicate.

In the sentence above 'plays cricket' is predicate. Predicate may be of one word or of more than one word.

> The birds fly.
> The leader of the party speaks aloud.
> They never come here without guns.
> The west wind blew very speedily.
> The decision to vote must be taken carefully.

In the above sentences the beginning part is called subject while the underlined part is called predicate. In the first sentence it is made of one word only while in the third it is made of five words.

Practice 1 Separate the subject and predicate in the following sentences-

(i) Dileep was searching his hen in the field.

(ii)The army defeated the invaders.

(iii) The poor are unhappy.

(iv) Whom god loves die young.

(v) Slow and steady wins the race.

(vi)The king's horses could not do that.

(vii)All the students of this university will have to appear in the test again.

(viii) The article of that newspaper emphasized the importance of Education.

(ix) The battle was won.

(x)The prince could not take decision early.

Answer-

	SUBJECT	PREDICATE
i	Dileep	was searching his hen in the field.
ii	The army	defeated the invaders.
iii	The poor	are unhappy.
iv	Whom god loves	die young.
v	Slow and steady	wins the race.
vi	The king's horses	could not do that.
vii	All the students of this university	will have to appear in the test again.
viii	The article of that newspaper	emphasized the importance of Education.
ix	The battle	was won.
x	The prince	could not take decision early.

There are different kinds of sentences: assertive or declarative sentences, interrogative sentences and imperative sentences.

While writing a sentence a few rules must be followed-

1. Always begin the sentence with a capital letter.

2. Follow the rules of subject verb agreement.
3. Use proper punctuation mark.

1.Assertive Sentences- Sentences which make simple assertions or statements are called assertive or declarative sentences. In these sentences the subject generally comes before the verb.

Examples-

Pink is my favorite color.
It is raining.
I go to morning walk every day.
I like watching TV.
These sentences may be positive or negative. Sentences which give a positive or affirmative sense are called **affirmative sentences.**

Honesty is the best policy.
I have seen the Taj.
Better late than never .

Sentences which give a negative meaning are called **negative sentences.**

He will not come here.
We should not disobey our elders.
2.Interrogative sentences- sentences which ask questions are called interrogative sentences.

What is your name?
Which game do you play?
Can you help me?
How do you go to school?

Wh-questions are made by wh-words and helping verbs.

What	do	you	play	?
What	does	he	sing	?
How	do	they	go	?
How	does	she	cook food	?
Where	do	we	study	?
When	does	he	stay	?
Which book	do	you	like	?
Why	do	I	take a ticket	?
Whose car	do	you	drive	?

What	are	you	playing	?
What	is	he	singing	?
How	are	they	performing	?
How	is	she	cooking food	?
Where	are	we	studying	?
When	is	he	staying	?
Which book	have	you	liked	?
Why	have	I	denied a ticket	?
What	has	he	purchased	?
Whose car	had	you	driven	?

Other questions (yes/no questions) begin with a helping verb/modal-

Do	you	like	sweets?
Does	he	take	tea?
Did	they	help	you?
Have	you	asked	your question?
Has	he	opened	the door?

Is	she	coming	here?
Am	I	taking	much time?
Are	we	going	to London?
Was	Raj	attending	the class?
Were	they	carrying	bags?
Will	you	wash	this room?
Shall	I	get	a letter?
Can	Geeta	lift	this suitcase?
Should	a man	bring	a bucket here?
Might	he	call	me?

3. Imperative sentences-Sentences which express orders, commands, requests, advice, proposals or suggestions are called imperative sentences.

Go out at once.(order)
Please listen to me.(request)
Work hard.(advice)
Let's play this game.(suggestion)

4. Exclamatory sentences-Sentences which express some strong feeling or emotion such as joy, sorrow, regret, surprise, wonder etc., are called exclamatory sentences.

What a marvelous site!
Hurrah! We have won the match.
Alas! She is dead.
How beautiful the place is!

Punctuation rules-

Assertive and imperative sentences are followed by a full stop.

Interrogative sentences are followed by a question mark.

Exclamatory sentences are followed by the sign of exclamation.

Practice 1: Identify the kind of these sentences:

1. What a beautiful dress!   3. Go out.
2. Why do you bring that bag?   4. These grapes are cheap.

5. Where do you go on Sunday? 6. I don't understand French.

3.1 Punctuation Marks

The marks or signs used in writing that divide sentences and phrases are called punctuation marks.

There are fourteen punctuation marks in English language. These are period (full stop), question mark, exclamation mark, comma, semicolon, colon, dash, hyphen, parentheses, brackets, braces, apostrophe, question marks, and ellipses.

The use of these punctuation marks is to be done judiciously.

Period (full stop), question mark and exclamation mark are used at the end of sentence.

Period (full stop)(.) -

- The period (full stop) is placed at the end of the complete statement, assertive sentence, imperative sentence or declarative sentence.

  The chief guest has arrived.
  I go to morning walk every day.
  Please listen to me.

- After an abbreviation also we put a full stop .For example- Govt., Imp.

Question Mark (?) – A question mark is used at the end of a sentence to indicate a direct question.

  When did you reach Mumbai?
  How did you open that box?

Are the passengers ready?

Exclamation mark (!) – The exclamation mark is used when a person wants to express a sudden feeling/emotion.

What a marvelous site!

Hurrah! We have won the match.

Alas! She is dead.

Comma, semicolon and colon are used to indicate pause in the series of words.

Comma (,)-

- The comma is used to separate the items in a list or to show that there is a little pause in a sentence.

    Example: I have some salt, a little sugar and two lemons.
              In that case, I guess I'll have to change the venue.
- In letters it is used after the salutation.

    Example: Dear Uncle,

Semicolon (;) – This mark is used to separate the parts of a complicated sentence or items in a detailed list ,showing a pause that is longer than a comma but shorter than a full stop.

Example- He kept the books in a bag carefully; he lifted the bag and started to walk toward the door.

She was disappointed; she knew that her friend wanted to mislead her by saying so.

Colon (:)-This mark is used to introduce a list, a summary, an explanation, etc. or before reporting what somebody has said. It is also used to separate out the hour and minute.

- It is 5:30 p.m.
- Hamlet: To be or not to be that is the question.

Dash (–) This mark is used to separate parts of a sentence often in place of a colon.

Bombay_ Guwahati train

 Hyphen (-) This mark is used to join two words together, to make a new one, as in 'get-together.' It is also used between the parts of a compound word or name.

Parentheses( ) This marked is used to give additional information about something/someone .It can also be replaced by a comma many times.

- Rahul and Seema (who were actually cousins) both went to see the movie that day.
- Ninety Forty Seven (the year of India's independence) is the most important year for Indian subcontinent.

Brackets [ ] These are used for technical explanations

Braces { } These marks are used to contain two or more lines of text or listed items to show that they are considered as a unit. These marks are often used in computer programming to show what should be contained within the same lines. These marks are also used in mathematics to put any number/algebraic quantities within bracket. The sequence of the bracket, braces and parentheses is as given below-

$$[2\{3(5+4)\}]$$

Ellipses (…) - These marks indicate omission, especially of letters or words. These marks are used often within quotations to jump from one phrase to another ,omitting unnecessary words.

Apostrophe (') This mark is used to indicate-

- Omission of a letter or letters from a word in making notes : An engineer'g college.
- The possessive case: Ram's ball, A boy's dress

Quotation Marks (" ") These are a pair of punctuation marks .These marks are used to mark the beginning and end of a passage/quotation taken from another author/source and are repeated word for word.

4. Tense

Verb is the most important part of a sentence. Verb tells about doing or happening of an action. Tense of a verb tells how and to what extent action has been completed.

There are three main verb tenses- present, past and future. Each main tense is divided into simple, progressive, perfect, and perfect progressive tenses.

	simple	**progressive**	**perfect**	**perfect progressive**
present	play	is/am/are playing	have/has played	have /has been playing.
past	played	was/were playing	had played	had been playing
future	will play	will be/shall be playing	will have/shall have played	will have been/shall have been playing.

Verbs in English have three forms. These are called present, past and past participle forms. A fourth form of verb is made by adding –ing in the verb .This form is called present participle form of a verb. To make sentences in various tenses knowledge of these forms of verb is very essential.

A few verbs with all four forms are given here.

Present/infinitive form	past form	past participle form	-ing form (present participle)
be	was/were	been	being
beat	beat	beaten	beating
begin	began	begun	beginning

bite	bit	bitten	biting
break	broke	broken	breaking
buy	bought	bought	buying
bring	brought	brought	bringing

Structure, use, hints and examples for each tense are given one by one.

4.1 Present Indefinite tense

Read this paragraph first:

Mr.Ramnarayan Shiva **works** in a multinational company in Noida. He **remains** very busy most of the time. He **gets up** early in the morning. He **goes** to morning walk to a nearby park. He **watches** TV news after coming back from there. His wife **goes to market** to buy vegetables. After it she **prepares** breakfast for him. They **take** breakfast together. He **moves** to office at about ten a.m. He **attends** meetings in the afternoon. He **advises** the officers on tricky matters. Their only son **works** in a bank in another city. He **lives** alone. He **comes** to meet Mr.Shiva at Diwali vacations every year. The family then **goes** to some tourist place .They **spend** their time living in ITC hotels. They **enjoy** their holidays.

Use-this tense is used to indicate an action in the present that takes place once, never, always or several times.

Hints: always, everyday, never, normally, often, seldom, sometimes, usually

There are two possibilities in the structure of a sentence of this tense.

Subject+ verb + object+ other words. [When the subject is I, We, You, They or other plural subject]

Subject+ verb+s/es + object+ other words. [When the subject is he/she/it or other singular subject]

Adding –s or –es in the verb: Generally –s is added in the verb when the subject is he/she/it or other singular subject except in the following conditions.

Example-

When the verb ends in sh , ch , ss , x, o ; we add -es	verb ending in –y • if verb has vowel before –y ,we add-s • if verb has consonant before –y ,we remove y and add –ies	
miss-misses catch-catches fix-fixes Wash-washes do-does	buy-buys say-says lay-lays stay-stays	fry-fries try-tries dry-dries carry-carries

Example sentences:

The affirmative sentences begin with the subject .The verb follows the subject. The sentences follow the pattern as given in the table. The first five sentences have first form of the verb. The last five sentences have verb+ s/es.

Subject	verb	Object	Remaining part of the sentence	Punctuation mark
I	read	a book	everyday	.
We	study	English	daily	.

You	take	tea	in the morning	.
They	come	to school	in the morning	.
The children	sing	a song	sometimes	.
He	buys	a pen	from the shop	.
She	washes	clothes	in the hostel	.
It	eats	grass	in the ground	.
Radha	writes	answers	with a pen	.
Mukesh	carries	a bag	on his shoulders	.

Practice 4.1A

Fill the suitable form of verb to make a sentence in present indefinite tense.

1. Dev ……………..tea. (take)
2. She …….. in a departmental store.(work)
3. We ………….. you for this help.(thank)
4. Teena ………….to get good marks in the test. (hope)
5. The scientists ……….. to make life easier.(try)

Practice 4.1B

Fill in the blanks with correct form of the verb-

(i)This magazine……….everything required.(contain/contains)
(ii) I ………….toys.(buy/buys)
(iii) The airplane………..late.(reach/reaches)
(iv) You ……….a flower pot.(carry/carries)
(v)His father …………the date of marriage.(fix/fixes)
(vi) Your daughter …………first division.(get/gets)
(vii)They…………for us.(wait/waits)
(viii)The child ……..loudly.(cry/cries)
(ix) One of the sheep ………..in this field.(graze/grazes)

Practice 4.1C

Fill in the blank with the right form of the verbs given in brackets:
(i)Rohit …………most of her afternoons in reading novels.(spend)
(ii)Deepak usually …………up at 6 o'clock in the morning .(get)
(iii) We don't …………cricket in winter.(play)
(iv) Dev always ………..the newspaper in the morning.(read)

(v)I never ....lies.(tell)

(vi)The sun ....in the west.(set)

(vii)The milkman ....milk daily.(bring)

(viii)Does your mother ....clothes before breakfast.(wash)

Present indefinite (interrogative sentences)

In order to make interrogative sentences of this tense we have to use helping verb Do/Does as helping verb in the beginning of the sentence. The sentence will end in question mark. The structure of sentences will be as per the table given here:

Helping verb	Subject	Main verb	Object	Remaining part	Punctuation mark
Do	I	read	a book	everyday	?
Do	we	study	English	daily	?
Do	you	take	tea	in the morning	?
Do	they	come	to school	in the morning	?
Do	the children	sing	a song	sometimes	?
Does	he	buy	a pen	from the shop	?
Does	she	wash	clothes	in the hostel	?
Does	it	eat	grass	in the ground	?
Does	Radha	write	answers	with a pen	?
Does	Mukesh	carry	a bag	on his shoulders	?

Practice 4.1D

Change into interrogative sentences (Yes/no questions).

1. He wants to have a lemon juice.
2. The children like cookies.
3. The teacher brings a duster.
4. She guides the passengers.
5. The train comes late every day.
6. I call him.
7. You bring bags.
8. We travel in summer.
9. They help their teachers.
10. The children call their mother.

Practice 4.1 E

Fill in the blanks with suitable helping verb:

1……he help you?(Do/Does)

2………you take tea?(Do/Does)

3……..she worry about homework?(Do/Does)

4……they visit here?(Do/Does)

5……we annoy you?(Do/Does)

6…. Raj play cricket?(Do/Does)

7…..Seema buy tickets?(Do/Does)

8……your mother tell you stories?(Do/Does)

9…..the postman ring the bell?(Do/Does)

10…..a cow move its tail?(Do/Does)

Wh-question in Present simple tense

What	do	you	play	?
What	does	he	sing	?
How	do	they	go	?
How	does	she	cook food	?
Where	do	we	study	?
When	does	he	stay	?
Which book	do	you	like	?
Why	do	I	take a ticket	?
Whose car	do	you	drive	?

Present Indefinite (Negative sentence)

To make a negative sentence in this tense we have to add do not or does not in between subject and verb. The first form of the verb is used here.

Subject	do not/ does not	verb	Object	Other words	Punctuati on mark
I	don't	read	a book	everyday	.
We	don't	study	English	daily	.
You	don't	take	tea	in the morning	.
They	don't	come	to school	in the morning	.
The children	don't	sing	a song	sometimes	.

He	doesn't	buys	a pen	from the shop	.
She	doesn't	wash	clothes	in the hostel	.
It	doesn't	eat	grass	in the ground	.
Radha	doesn't	write	answers	with a pen	.
Mukesh	doesn't	carry	a bag	on his shoulders	.

Present Indefinite (Negative Interrogative) sentences:

Do/Does + Subject +not +verb+ object/remaining part of the sentence.

Does	he	not	take tea?
Do	you	not	like mangoes?
Does	she	not	dance?
Do	I	not	help you?
Where do	they	not	read stories?
Do	I	not	come in time?

Practice 4.1F

Change into negative sentences-

1. I believe in his story.
2. The officers attend the meeting.
3. That shopkeeper opens the shop.
4. This toy works well.
5. His car moves smoothly.

6. Your father works in an office.
7. His kite flies high.
8. He opens this shop early.
9. She calls her friends.
10. The government imposes the tax.

Practice 4.1 G

Fill in the blanks with don't /doesn't.

1. He ………..help his brother.
2. I ………..like coffee.

3. You …………..bring any bag.
4. She ………..speak any words.

5. Raju ......pick rags.

6. The manager.....visit the hotel.
7. It....rain here in July.

8. My uncle.....Polish his shoes.
9. The train........stop here.
10. The driver .....stop at the bus stop.

Practice 4.1H

Change these sentences into negative interrogative sentences-

a. Rahul drives a car.
b. He explain the reason of his absence.
c. The people neglect their duties towards environment.
d. We donate blood in blood bank every year.
e. The elephant uses its trunk for spreading water.
f. It rains heavily in this area.
g. The birds migrate to other part of the world in winter.
h. Her mother advises her to keep her cell phone charged.
i. The train comes late in foggy mornings.
j. The customers have given preference to this product.

Practice 4.1 I

Change these sentences into negative and interrogative sentences. The first one is done for you.

1. Mr.Ramnarayan Shiva works in a multinational company in Noida.
Negative   : Mr.Narayan Shiva does not work in a multinational company.
Interrogative: Does Mr.Narayan Shiva work in a multinational company?
2. He remains very busy most of the time.
Negative   : ....
Interrogative: ....
3. He gets up early in the morning.
Negative   : ....
Interrogative: ....
4. He goes to morning walk to a nearby park.
Negative   : ....
Interrogative: ....
5. He watches TV news after coming back from there.
Negative   : ....

152

Interrogative: ....

     6. His wife **goes to market** to buy vegetables.

Negative   : ....

Interrogative: ....

     7. She **prepares** breakfast for him.

Negative   : ....

Interrogative: ....

     8. They take breakfast together.

Negative   : ....

Interrogative: ....

     9. He moves to office at about ten a.m.

Negative   : ....

Interrogative: ....

     10. He attends meetings in the afternoon.

Negative   : ....

Interrogative: ....

     11. He advises the officers on tricky matters.

Negative   : ....

Interrogative: ....

     12. Their only son works in a bank in another city.

Negative   : ....

Interrogative: ....

     13. He lives alone.

Negative   : ....

Interrogative: ....

     14. He comes to meet Mr.Shiva at Diwali vacations every year.

Negative   : ....

Interrogative: :...

     15. The family then goes to some tourist place .

Negative   : ....

Interrogative: ....

     16. They spend their time living in ITC hotels.

Negative   : ....

Interrogative: ....

     17. They enjoy their holidays.

Negative   : ....

Interrogative: ....

4.2 Past Indefinite Tense

Let us read this story first:

The school **opened** after summer vacation. The students **requested** their parents to buy new books and copies. The shopkeeper **became** busy. The stationery shops **filled** with copies, pencil boxes, books and other items. The cloth merchants **focused** on school dresses. The school bag dealers **stored** bags for every age group. The roads **filled** with school buses. The daily routine of students **changed.** Now the day **started** with the thought of homework. The homework **became** the priority of the children. They **reduced** watching cartoon shows.

Use-This tense is used to express an action that happened or completed in past, usually a very little time before speaking, or action which is just completed.

Hints: yesterday, 3 minutes ago, in 2000, the other day, last Sunday

Structure- Subject+ second form of verb + object+ remaining part.

Example:

- He **came** to my home yesterday.
- I have **turned** off the computer 3 minutes ago.
- They **worked** in New York in 2000.
- She **complained** about the weather the other day.
- You **asked** a question yesterday.
- Deepak **refused** to go there.
- Amit **handled** the situation very well.
- His mother **helped** him in homework.

subject	second form of verb	object	remaining part	full stop
I	took	tea	in the morning	.
We	studied	English	daily	.
You	carried	a bag	on his shoulders	.
They	completed	homework	late yesterday.	.
The servants	ate	bananas	from the table	.
Kari	helped	the drowning boy	in the river	.
The king	declared	the award	for answers	.
He	went	to the hut	of the hermit.	.
She	washed	clothes	on Saturday	.
It	drank	water	through its trunk	.
The wise men	gave	different answers	to king's questions	.

Practice 4.2 A

Fill the suitable form of the verb to make sentences of past simple tense.

1. He .... his umbrella. (Forget)
2. They.............. this news with shock.(Listen)
3. Ruby ....the morning train. (Catch)

4. Michael ………… the idea. (Like)

5. The newspaper …………the city in detail. (Describe)

Practice 4.2 B

Select the right form of the verb to make a sentence of past simple tense.

1. Ram ………..a letter. (Write/wrote/written)

2. He ……….......tea. (take /took/taken)

3. They………...me. (help/helped/helped)

4. You ……..…...in time.(arrive)

5. The airplane …..……. in the sky. (fly/flew/flown)

6. The buffalo …………..milk. (give/gave/given)

7. The milkman ………....milk. (sell/sold)

8. I ……….......the tour. (cancel/cancelled)

9. We…………some clothes. (wash/washed)

10. Deepak…….the gate. (open/opened)

Past indefinite (negative sentences)

To make negative sentence of this tense we use helping verb did not in all kind of subjects. After the helping verb the base form of the verb is used.

Structure: subject + did not+ first form of the verb+ object.

subject	did not	base form of verb	object	remaining part	.
I	did not	take	tea	in the morning	.
We	did not	study	English	daily	.
You	did not	carry	a bag	on his shoulders	.
They	did not	complete	homework	yesterday.	.
He	did not	go	to the hut	of the hermit.	.
She	did not	wash	clothes	on Saturday	.
It	did not	drink	water	through its trunk	.
The wise	did not	give	answers	to king's	.

156

men				questions	

Practice 4.2C

Change into negative sentences-
1. He completed his homework in the evening.
2. The government proposed a new tax.
3. Rajkumar washed a shirt.
4. You attended the lecture of Mr. Johnson.
5. The birds flew away.
6. The kite reached high.

Past indefinite (interrogative sentences)

Helping verb	subject	First form of verb	object	remaining part	punctuation mark
Did	I	take	tea	in the morning	?
Did	we	study	English	daily	?
Did	you	carry	a bag	on your back	?
Did	they	complete	homework	late	?
Did	the servants	eat	bananas	from the table	?
Did	the tourist	help	the drowning boy	in the river	?
Did	the king	declare	the award	for answers	?
Did	he	go	to the hut	of the hermit.	?
Did	she	wash	clothes	on Saturday	?
Did	Jumbo	drink	water	through its trunk	?
Did	The wise men	give	different answers	to king's questions	?

Practice 4.2 D

Change these sentences into negative and interrogative sentences. The first one is done for you.

1. The school **opened** after summer vacation.
Negative   : The school did not open after summer vacation.
Interrogative: Did the schools open after summer vacation?
2. The students **requested** their parents to buy new books and copies.
Negative   : ....
Interrogative: ....

3. The shopkeeper **became** busy.
Negative   : ....
Interrogative: ....
4.The stationary shops **filled** with copies.
Negative   : ....
Interrogative: ....
5. The cloth merchants focused on school dresses.
Negative   : ....
Interrogative: ....
6.The school bag dealers stored bags for every age group.
Negative   : ....
Interrogative: ....
7. The roads filled with school buses.
Negative   : ....
Interrogative: ....
8.The daily routine of students changed.
Negative   : ....
Interrogative: ....
9. Now the day started with the thought of homework.
Negative   : ....
Interrogative: ....
10. The homework became the priority of the children.
Negative   : ....
Interrogative: ....
11. They reduced watching cartoon shows.
Negative   : ....
Interrogative: ....

4.3 Future Simple Tense

Let us read this story before going further:

The train **will arrive** soon. It **will stop** at the station. The passengers **will become** active. They **will choose** the right coach. The children **will show** their happiness. The elders **will be** cautious. The coolies **will help** the passengers in keeping the luggage inside the coaches. The passengers **will take** their seats. The train **will start** after a few minutes. The Station master **will show** the green flag. The guard **will blow** the whistle. The wheels of the train **will start** rotating. The smoke **will appear** rising up from the engine. The tree beside the track **will appear** moving backwards. Then I **shall open** my bag. You **will ask** for a biscuit. **We shall** enjoy eating the sweet cookies on the way.

This tense tells about an action in the future or assumption with regard to future.

Hints - in a year, next month, tomorrow, in the evening

Structure: Subject +shall/will +first form of the verb+ object+ remaining part of the sentence.

With 'I' and 'we' helping verb 'shall' is used. With remaining subjects we use 'will' as helping verb.

subject	helping verb	main verb	remaining part	punctuation mark

I	shall	go	to school	.
we	shall	play	cricket	.
You	will	get	a copy	.
They	will	come	here.	.
The girls	will	clean	the door.	.
He	will	swim	in the river	.
She	will	complete	her homework	.
The elephant	will	chew	twigs and leaves	.
His friend	will	come	out of water	.

Negative Sentences:

Structure: Subject +shall/will +first form of the verb+ object+ remaining part of the sentence.

subject	helping verb	not	main verb	remaining part	.
I	shall	not	go	to school	.
we	shall	not	play	cricket	.
You	Will	not	get	a copy	.
They	will	not	come	here.	.
The girls	will	not	clean	the door.	.
He	will	not	swim	in the river	.
She	will	not	complete	her homework	.
The elephant	will	not	chew	twigs and leaves	.
His friend	will	not	come	out of water	.

Interrogative Sentences:

Structure: Shall/will + Subject + first form of the verb+ object+ remaining part of the sentence.

Helping verb	Subject	Not	Main verb	Remaining part	?
shall	I		not	go	to school	?

shall	we	not	play	cricket	?
Will	you	not	get	a copy	?
will	they	not	come	here.	?
will	the girls	not	clean	the door.	?
will	he	not	swim	in the river	?
will	she	not	complete	her homework	?
will	the elephant	not	chew	twigs and leaves	?
will	his friend	not	come	out of water	?

We can get the same meaning by using is going to/am going to /are going to in place of will /shall.

I	am	going to	buy	a car.
He/ She/It/Raj	is	going to	receive	biscuits.
We /You/They/ Raj and Komal	are	going to	reach	the market soon.

Practice 4.3 A

Fill in the blanks with **is going/am going to/are going to.**

1. I ……………..buy a new bicycle.
2. You ………….get good marks in the Examination.
3. She ………….receive a lot gift in her birthday.
4. The teacher………… organize a class test soon.
5. We……………..face a lot of problems due to power failure.
6. They ………….bring a big suitcase for the whole family.
7. Ajeet ………….open a big shop in the coming July.
8. It………………...get a new belt for its neck tomorrow.
9. The public ………...utilize the facility of ATMs very soon.
10. The car …………cross 70000 kilometers till next month.

Practice 4.3B

Change these sentences into negative and interrogative sentences. The first one is done for you.

1. The train **will arrive** soon.
Negative   : The train **will not arrive** soon.
Interrogative: Will the train **arrive** soon?

2. It will stop at the station.
Negative   : ....
Interrogative: ....

3. The passengers will become active.
Negative   : ....
Interrogative: ....

4. They will choose the right coach.
Negative   : ....
Interrogative: ....

5. The children will show their happiness.
Negative   : ....
Interrogative: ....

6. The elders will be cautious.
Negative   : ....
Interrogative: ....

7. The coolies will help the passengers in keeping the luggage inside the coaches.
Negative   : ....
Interrogative: ....

8. The passengers will take their seats.
Negative   : ....
Interrogative: ....

9. The train will start after a few minutes.
Negative   : ....
Interrogative: ....

10. The Station master will show the green flag.
Negative   : ....
Interrogative: ....

11. The guard will blow the whistle.
Negative   : ....

Interrogative: …………………………….....

      12.The wheels of the train will start rotating.

Negative   : …………………………….

Interrogative: …………………………….....

      13.The smoke will appear rising up from the engine.

Negative   : …………………………….

Interrogative: …………………………….....

      14.The tree beside the track will appear moving backwards.

Negative   : …………………………….

Interrogative: …………………………….....

      15.I shall open my bag.

 Negative   : …………………………….

Interrogative: …………………………….....

      16. You will ask for a biscuit.

Negative   : …………………………….

Interrogative: …………………………….....

      17. We shall enjoy eating the sweet cookies on the way.

Negative   : …………………………….

Interrogative: …………………………….....

4.4 Present Continuous Tense

Let us see this story:

Now Surabhi is in her house. She **is sitting** on a plastic chair. She **is holding** a book. She is reading it.

Atul is Surabhi's husband. He **is sitting** in front of her. He **is reading** a newspaper.

Both Surabhi and Atul **are reading** something.

Divya **is sitting** next to Atul. She is Surabhi's sister. Right now she **is talking** to Surabhi and Atul.

At this moment a boy **is coming** in. He **is wearing** white clothes. He **is carrying** a letter in his hand. He is reading the letter.

This tense is used to express an action that is in progress at the moment of speaking.

Hints-at the moment, just now, right now.

Structure: Subject+ helping verb (is/am/are) +ing form of verb + object+ other words

Examples:

1. They are traveling by train.
2. He is driving a car.

3. I am waiting for the newspaper.

4. You are sitting on a wooden bench.

5. We are thinking about our next picnic.

6. Rajesh is helping his brother in packing the bags.

7. Her mother is cooking food for him in the kitchen.

8. Their teacher is writing something on the blackboard.

9. The headmaster is sitting with other teachers in the office.

10. The birds are flying in the sky.

Some other examples of affirmative sentences:

Subject	Helping verb	Verb+ ing	Remaining part	Full stop
I	am	sitting	on an elephant	.
we	are	reading	a lesson	.
You	are	talking	to me	.
They	are	digging	the ground	.
The wise men	are	giving	advises	.
Hermit and the king	are	working	in the field	.
He	is	lying	on the bed	.
She	is	asking	questions	.
An ant	is	laying	eggs	.
The captain	is	going	somewhere	.
The plant	is	growing	into an tree	.

Negative Sentences:

Structure: Subject+ helping verb (is/am/are) +not+ ing form of verb + object+ other words

Subject	Helping verb	not	Verb + ing	Remaining part	.
I	am	not	sitting	on an elephant	.
we	are	not	reading	a lesson	.

You	are	not	talking	to me	.
They	are	not	digging	the ground	.
The wise men	are	not	giving	advices	.
Hermit and the king	are	not	working	in the field	.
He	is	not	lying	on the bed	.
She	is	not	asking	questions	.
An ant	is	not	laying	eggs	.
The captain	is	not	going	somewhere	.
The plant	is	not	growing	into an tree	.

Interrogative Sentences:

Structure: Helping verb (is/am/are) +Subject + ing form of verb + object+ other words

Helping verb	Subject	Verb+ ing	Remaining part	?
Am	I	sitting	on an elephant	?
Are	we	reading	a lesson	?
Are	you	talking	to me	?
Are	they	digging	the ground	?
Are	the wise men	giving	advises	?
Are	hermit and the king	working	in the field	?
Is	he	lying	on the bed	?
Is	she	asking	questions	?
Is	an ant	laying	eggs	?
Is	the captain	going	somewhere	?
Is	the plant	growing	into an tree	?

Practice4.4A

Fill in the blanks with suitable helping verb (is/am/are) to make sentences of present continuous tense.

1. I ……waiting for my friend.
2. She……washing plates in the kitchen.
3. He …….playing with a toy.
4. Rajiv …….waiting for your reply.
5. They………..sitting with some foreigners.
6. We………….planning a holiday.
7. Dinesh and Rahul………going to London.
8. Your mother …….driving a car.
9. It…….raining heavily outside.
10. The birds ………chirping in the woods.
11. The cows of my neighbour ……….grazing in the field.
12. The stars………shining in the sky.
13. The meeting of the directors ………going on.
14. The people …….protesting against price hike.
15. My friends ……. celebrating the new year in a hotel.

Practice 4.4B

Change these sentences into negative and interrogative sentences. The first one is done for you.

1. She **is sitting** on a plastic chair.
Negative   : She **is not sitting** on a plastic chair.
Interrogative: Is she **sitting** on a plastic chair.
2. She is holding a book.
Negative   : ……………………………..
Interrogative: ……………………………..
3. She is reading it.
Negative   : ……………………………..
Interrogative: ……………………………..
4. He is sitting in front of her.
Negative   : ………………………………

Interrogative: ....

     5. He is reading a newspaper.

Negative   : ....

Interrogative: ....

     6. Both Surabhi and Atul are reading something.

Negative   : ....

Interrogative: ....

     7. Divya is sitting next to Atul.

Negative   : ....

Interrogative: ....

     8. Right now she is talking to Surabhi and Atul.

Negative   : ....

Interrogative: ....

     9. At this moment a boy is coming in.

Negative   : ....

Interrogative: ....

     10.He is wearing white clothes.

Negative   : ....

Interrogative: ....

     11. He is carrying a letter in his hand.

Negative   : ....

Interrogative: ....

     12. He is reading the letter.

Negative   : ....

Interrogative: ....

4.5 Past Continuous Tense

Let us read a story first.

Yesterday it **was raining** heavily. Ruby **was playing** inside the drawing room. She wanted to go outside. But her mother **was not allowing** her to go out. Ruby **was feeling** bored inside the house.

Ruby **was trying** to keep herself busy. She **was turning** the pages of a kid's magazine. After that she brought out her toy car. She **was playing** with that car till lunch time. After lunch she went to the next room to watch TV.

While she **was watching** TV the door bell rang. Her brother came holding an umbrella. He **was wearing** high shoes. He brought a comic book from the market.

While they **were watching** the comic book the rain stopped. But Ruby did not want to go out now. She **was enjoying** the comic book with her brother.

This tense is used to talk about action that was going on at a certain time in the past or things that were in progress in the past.

Hint words-when, while, last year, yesterday

Structure- Subject+ helping verb (was/were) + ing form of verb + object+ remaining part.

Example-

1. They were taking tca.
2. I was watching TV when she called.
3. While I was writing the email, the computer suddenly went off.

Subject	Helping verb`	Verb+ ing	Remaining part	Full stop
I	was	singing	a song	.
We	were	dancing	on the floor.	.
You	were	going	there	.
They	were	jumping	on the ground	.
He	was	carrying	a bag	.
She	was	stealing	an apple	.
It	was	waiting for	him	.
Raj	was	speaking	English	.
Meena	was	watching	a film	.
Raj and Meena	were	washing	clothes	.
The children	were	searching	a cat	.
The people	were	moving	in the market	.

Negative Sentences:

Structure- Subject+ helping verb (was/were) +not+ ing form of verb + object/ remaining part.

Subject	Helping verb`	not	Verb+ ing	object/ Remaining part	.

I	was	not	singing	a song	.
We	were	not	dancing	on the floor.	.
You	were	not	going	there	.
They	were	not	jumping	on the ground	.
He	was	not	carrying	a bag	.
She	was	not	stealing	an apple	.
It	was	not	waiting for	him	.
Raj	was	not	speaking	English	.
Meena	was	not	watching	a film	.
Raj and Meena	were	not	washing	clothes	.
The children	were	not	searching	a cat	.
The people	were	not	moving	in the market	.

Interrogative Sentences:

Structure- Helping verb (was/were) + subject + ing form of verb + object/ remaining part

| Was | I/he/she /it/Raj | singing | a song | ? |
| Were | we/you/they/the children | reading | a newspaper | ? |

Practice 4.5A

Fill in the blanks with suitable helping verb to make sentences of past continuous tense.

1. He.......waiting for you. (was/were)
2. They ....standing outside. (was/were)
3. Dileep ....buying tickets. (was/were)
4. Our teacher ....explaining us Newton's first law. (was/were)
5. Her friend......calling her on phone. (was/were)
6. I............. arranging the boxes properly. (was/were)
7. We........travelling in a train.(was/were)
8. The postman ....riding a bicycle.(was/were)
9. His mother......... cooking something special for her.(was/were)

10. Their father ………..worrying about their result.(was/were)

Practice 4.5 B

Complete the sentences using the past continuous tense form of the verb given in the bracket.

1. He …………. (wash) his car all yesterday afternoon.
2. I ………….. (read) a novel when the door bell rang.
3. They…………(get) ready to go to the station when the electricity turned off.
4. The gardener ………..(trim) the branches of the tree when the rain started.
5. At 8p.m. yesterday they………….(enjoy) dinner with their friends.
6. This morning he………..(listen) music in the drawing room.
7. Last Sunday we …………..(swim) in the pond.
8. Yesterday evening your friend ………..(drive) a car on the highway.

Practice 4.5 C

Change these sentences into negative and interrogative sentences. The first one is done for you.

1. Yesterday it **was raining** .
Negative   : Yesterday it **was not raining**.
Interrogative: Was it **raining** yesterday?
2. Ruby was playing inside the drawing room.
Negative   : ………………………………………
Interrogative: ………………………………………...
3. Ruby was feeling bored inside the house.
Negative   : ………………………………………
Interrogative: ………………………………………...
4. Ruby was trying to keep herself busy.
Negative   : ………………………………………
Interrogative: ………………………………………...
5. She was turning the pages of a kid's magazine.
Negative   : ………………………………………

Interrogative: ……………………………………...
      6. He was wearing high shoes.
Negative   : ……………………………………
Interrogative: ……………………………………
      7. They were watching the comic book.
Negative   : ……………………………………
Interrogative: ……………………………………...
      8. She was enjoying the comic book.
Negative   : ……………………………………
Interrogative: ……………………………………...

4.6 Future continuous tense

Let us read this story first:

In the evening we **shall be traveling** by train to Bhopal. We shall reach the station before 5.00 pm. The passengers **will be buying** tickets at the station. The Ticket checkers **will be checking** tickets at the gates. The tea sellers **will be calling** for customers.
When the train will reach Bhopal, some passengers **will be coming out** of the coaches. Others **will be waiting** for their stations to come. We **will be hiring** some auto rickshaw to reach our aunt's home.

This tense is used to express an action that is going on at a certain time in the future.

Hints-in one year, next week, tomorrow

Structure:

Subject+ Will/Shall + ing form of verb+ object/remaining part

Subject	Helping verb	Verb+ ing	object/remaining part	Punctuation mark
I	shall be	singing	a song	.

We	shall be	dancing	on the floor.	.
You	will be	going	there	.
They	will be	jumping	on the ground	.
He	will be	carrying	a bag	.
She	will be	stealing	an apple	.
It	will be	raining	in New York	.
Raj	will be	speaking	English	.
Meena	will be	watching	a film	.
Raj and Meena	will be	washing	clothes	.
The children	will be	searching	a cat	.
The people	will be	moving	in the market	.

Negative Sentences:

Structure:

Subject+ Will/Shall +not +be+ ing form of verb+ object/remaining part

Subject	Will not be /shall not be	Verb+ ing	object/remaining part	Punctuation mark
I	shall not be	singing	a song	.
we	shall not be	dancing	on the floor.	.
You	will not be	going	there	.
They	will not be	jumping	on the ground	.
He	will not be	carrying	a bag	.
She	will not be	stealing	an apple	.
It	will not be	raining	in New York	.
Raj	will not be	speaking	English	.

Interrogative Sentences:

Structure:

Will/Shall + Subject+ be+ ing form of verb+ object/remaining part ?

174

Shall/Will	Subject	be	Verb+ ing	object/ remaining part	Punctuation mark
Shall	I	be	singing	a song	?
Shall	we	be	dancing	on the floor.	?
Will	you	be	going	there	?
Will	they	be	jumping	on the ground	?
Will	he	be	carrying	a bag	?
Will	she	be	stealing	an apple	?
Will	it	be	raining	in New York	?
Will	Raj	be	speaking	English	?

Practice 4.6 A

Put the correct form of the verb to make sentences of future continuous tense.

1. This evening we ……….. a movie.(watch)
2. Tomorrow morning we……….. (work).
3. He………… (listen) a song.
4. I ………… (read) a novel this afternoon.
5. They ……….. (argue)again.
6. She………….. (do)homework tomorrow morning.
7. You……….. (walk) this evening.
8. Mr.Sharma………… (open) his shop tomorrow morning.
9. We ……….. (wait)for you at the Railway station.
10. The government………… (impose) some new taxes next March.

Practice 4.6 B

Change these sentences into negative and interrogative sentences. The first one is done for you.

1. We **shall be traveling** by train to Bhopal.

Negative : **We shall not be travelling by train to Bhopal.**

175

Interrogative: Shall we be travelling by train to Bhopal ?

2. We shall reach the station before 5.00 pm.

Negative : ....

Interrogative: ....

3. The passengers will be buying tickets at the station.

Negative : ....

Interrogative: ....

4. The Ticket checkers will be checking tickets at the gates.

Negative : ....

Interrogative: ....

5. The tea sellers will be calling for customers.

Negative : ....

Interrogative: ....

6. Some passengers will be coming out of the coaches.

Negative : ....

Interrogative: ....

7. We will be hiring some auto rickshaw to reach our aunt's home.

Negative : ....

Interrogative: ....

4.7 Present perfect tense

Let us read this story first:

Kokila **has just come inside** the house from the courtyard. **She has put on** a sari. She **has finished** washing clothes. She **has also spread** the clothes in a line for drying.

Now Deepali and Aunt are outside. Deepali **has just come back** from a friend's house. She **has seen** a new dress there. Recently, Aunt **has moved** in with Deepali's family. She now enjoys living with them.

Aunt **has** already **sat** down in a chair. She also wears a sari. She **has** just **finished** drying her hair.

This tense is used to express an action that stopped recently. It is a finished Action that has influence on the present.

Hints-already, ever, just, never, not yet, so far, till now, up to now

Examples:

- Radheshyam has opened a shop.
- She has opened a window.
- I have finished my homework.
- Have you seen the Taj?

177

- They have not received tickets.

Structure: Subject+ have/has+ third form of the verb+ object /remaining part.

Subject	helping verb	third form of the main verb	object/ remaining part of the sentence.	
I	have	seen	the Taj	.
we	have	completed	the work	.
You	have	washed	clothes	.
They	have	reached	Bhopal	.
He	has	bought	a copy	.
She	has	caught	a bird	.
It	has	eaten	a mango.	.
Raj	has	sent	a letter	.
Meena	has	watched	a film	.
Raj and Meena	have	written	a poem	.
The children	have	played	a match	.
The people	have	bought	vegetables	.

Negative Sentences:

Formula: S+ has/have+ not+ third form of the verb+ object/remaining part.

Subject	helping verb	not	third form of the main verb	object/ remaining part of the sentence.	
I	have	not	seen	the Taj	.
we	have	not	completed	the work	.
You	have	not	washed	clothes	.
They	have	not	reached	Bhopal	.
He	has	not	bought	a copy	.
She	has	not	caught	a bird	.
It	has	not	eaten	a mango.	.

Raj	has	not	sent	a letter		.

Interrogative Sentences:

Formula: Has/Have+ subject + third form of the verb+ object/remaining part?

Helping verb	Subject	third form of the main verb	object/ remaining part of the sentence.	?
Have	I	seen	the Taj	?
Have	we	completed	the work	?
Have	you	washed	clothes	?
Have	they	reached	Bhopal	?
Has	he	bought	a copy	?
Has	she	caught	a bird	?
Has	it	eaten	a mango.	?
Has	Raj	sent	a letter	?

PRACTICE 4.7 A

Fill in the blanks with suitable form of verbs to make sentences of present perfect tense.

1.I ………..(see) this movie many times.
2. My friends ………..(use) my guitar several times.
3.Daisy ………..(finish)her drawing.
4.I ………………(eat)four bananas.
5.She ……………(pay) the bill.
6.He …………..(accept)his mistake.
7.You……………(sell) seven T-Shirts till now.
8.Rajkumar ………..(wear) that shirt on many occasions.
9.The police…………..(arrest) the thief.
10.The Court ………………(deliver) the judgment.

PRACTICE 4.7 B

Fill in the blanks with suitable form of verbs to make sentences of present perfect tense.

1. I /study/English.
2. She/eat/apples.
3. They/go/temple.
4. We/read/that /movie.
5. She/lose/her keys.
6. I /miss/the train.
7. My mother/cook/breakfast.
8. You /find/the address.
9. I /meet/Rohit
10. The girl/complain/to the police.

Practice 4.7 C

Change these sentences into negative and interrogative sentences. The first one is done for you.

1. Kokila **has come inside** the house from the courtyard.

Negative : Kokila **has not come** inside the house from the courtyard.
Interrogative: Has Kokila **come** inside the house from the courtyard?

2. **She has put on** a sari.
Negative : ....
Interrogative: ....
3. She **has finished** washing clothes.
Negative : ....
Interrogative: ....
4. She **has spread** the clothes in a line for drying.
Negative : ....
Interrogative: ....
5. Deepali **has just come back** from a friend's house.
Negative : ....
Interrogative : ....
6. She **has seen** a new dress there.
Negative : ....
Interrogative: ....

      7. Aunt **has moved** in with Deepali's family.

Negative   : ....

Interrogative: ....

      8. Aunt **has sat** down in a chair.

Negative   : ....

Interrogative: ....

      9. She **has** just **finished** drying her hair.

Negative   : ....

Interrogative: ....

4.8 Past Perfect Tense

Let us read this story first:

I visited Agra last year. Before that I **had** never **seen** such a beautiful building. I **had booked** the tickets two months earlier. I was very excited to see the Taj Mahal. Before my trip to Agra, I **had** never **been** outside Madhya Pradesh.

When I reached Agra, I spent many days visiting various places of the city. The city is historical. I **had read** about its history in books before planning to go there.

By the time I left Agra, I **had toured** many historical places. Fatehpur Sikri, Agra Fort, Mehtab Bagh, and Shees Mahal were just a few of the places I saw. Before this visit I **had** only **seen** these places in TV shows.

This tense is used to speak about an action that took place before a certain time in the past.

Hints- already, just, never, not yet, once, until that day

Structure: Subject +had+ past participle form of the verb+ object.

Subject	had	third form of the verb	object/remaining part	
I	had	seen	the Taj	.
we	had	completed	the work	.
You	had	washed	clothes	.
They	had	reached	Bhopal	.
He	had	bought	a copy	.
She	had	caught	a bird	..
It	had	eaten	a mango.	.
Raj	had	sent	a letter	.
Meena	had	watched	a film	.
Raj and Meena	had	written	a poem	.
The children	had	played	a match	.
The people	had	bought	vegetables	.

Negative Sentence:

Formula: S+ had+ not+ third form of the verb+ object/remaining part of the verb.

Subject	had	not	third form of the verb	object/remaining part	.
I	had	not	seen	the Taj	.
we	had	not	completed	the work	.
You	had	not	washed	clothes	.
They	had	not	reached	Bhopal	.
He	had	not	bought	a copy	.
She	had	not	caught	a bird	.
It	had	not	eaten	a mango.	.
Raj	had	not	sent	a letter	.
Raj and Meena	had	not	written	a poem	.

Interrogative Sentence:

Formula: Had+ S+ third form of the verb+ object/remaining part of the verb?

Had	Subject	third form of the verb	object/remaining part	?
Had	I	seen	the Taj	?
Had	we	completed	the work	?
Had	you	washed	clothes	?
Had	they	reached	Bhopal	?
Had	he	bought	a copy	?
Had	she	caught	a bird	?
Had	it	eaten	a mango.	?
Had	Raj	sent	a letter	?
Had	Raj and Meena	written	a poem	?

Practice 4.8A

1. He…………….(never talk) to a girl, so he …………(be) embarrassed.
2. She ………..(never travel)by train before selection in a boarding school.
3. When she……… (call),I ………………(go) to sleep.
4. They…………….(tell) us they …………(renovate) the entire building.
5.The Manager……..(inform)us that he…..(appoint)a computer operator.
6. I ……….. (save) a lot of money before I ……..(buy) that restaurant.
7. I……………… (never be) to Delhi till 2008.
8. Before I ………… (take) final decision I ………..(read) more details.
9. He had………… (have) all the documents but he……….. (lose) them.
10. When I ……….. (reach) the station the train ………..(leave)

Practice 4.8 B

1. The thief ……………..before the police arrived.(run away)
2. They faced a lot of questions of ticket checker because they ………..their tickets.(lose)
3. The driver ………………the car before he started it. (wash)
4. We ……………them before we reached their home.(inform)
5. He …………….a lot before he appeared in the test.(practice)
6. The train …………..the station before we reached the station.(leave)

7. You ………….in Bangalore for 2 years before you shifted to Nagpur.(be)

8. Ajeet …………..very sick until he stopped drinking.(be)

9. The actor …………..many hardships before he finally got success.(go through)

10. She …………….to Paris before 2012.(be)

Answer- 1.had run away 2.had lost 3.had washed 4.had informed 5. had practiced 6.had left 7. had been 8.had been 9.had gone through 10.had been

Practice 4.8 C

Change these sentences into negative /affirmative and interrogative. The first one has been done for you.

    1. I **had** never **seen** such a beautiful building.

Affirmative   : I had seen such a beautiful building.

Interrogative : Had I seen such a beautiful building?

    2. I had booked the tickets two months earlier.

Negative   : …………………………………………...

Interrogative : …………………………………………...

    3. I had never been outside Madhya Pradesh.

Affirmative : …………………………………………...

Interrogative : …………………………………………...

    4. I had read about its history in books before planning to go there.

Negative   : …………………………………………...

Interrogative : …………………………………………...

    5. I had toured many historical places.

Negative : …………………………………………...

Interrogative : …………………………………………...

    6. Before this visit I had only seen these places in TV shows.

Negative : …………………………………………...

Interrogative : …………………………………………...

4.9 Future Perfect Tense

Let us read this story first:

Amit works in a bakery. He prepares the cakes there. He works form morning to evening. By the time he finishes working today, he **will have worked** 7 hours. He **will have baked** 25 cakes till evening.

Rakesh also works in the bakery. Next month he **will have completed** 2 years of his service there. By the time he goes to take lunch today, he **will have worked** for 3 hours. Till evening he **will have baked** 32 cakes today.

Both Amit and Rakesh live in a rented house. They have planned to buy a new house together. Till next year they **will have shifted** in their own house.

This tense is used to tell about an action that is completed at a certain time in the future.

Hints-next month, next year, in 2150

Structure: Subject +shall have/will have+ past participle form of verb + object.

Subject	Will have/Shall have	Third form of the verb	Object/Remaining part.	
I	shall have	seen	the Taj	.
we	shall have	completed	the work	.
You	will have	washed	clothes	.
They	will have	reached	Bhopal	.
He	will have	bought	a copy	.
She	will have	caught	a bird	..
It	will have	eaten	a mango.	.
Raj	will have	sent	a letter	.

185

Raj and Meena	will have	written	a poem	.

Negative Sentences:

Formula: Subject +shall not have/ will not have+ past participle form of verb + object.

Subject	Will not have/Shall not have	Third form of the verb	Object/Remaining part.	
I	shall not have	seen	the Taj	.
we	shall not have	completed	the work	.
You	will not have	washed	clothes	.
They	will not have	reached	Bhopal	.
He	will not have	bought	a copy	.
She	will not have	caught	a bird	..
It	will not have	eaten	a mango.	.
Raj	will not have	sent	a letter	.
Raj and Meena	will not have	written	a poem	.

Interrogative Sentences:

Formula: Shall /Will + S+ have+ past participle form of verb + object/remaining part of the sentence+ question mark

Will/Shall	Subject	have	Third form of the verb	Object/ Remaining part.	?
Shall	I	have	seen	the Taj	?
Shall	we	have	completed	the work	?
Will	you	have	washed	clothes	?
Will	they	have	reached	Bhopal	?
Will	he	have	bought	a copy	?
Will	she	have	caught	a bird	?
Will	it	have	eaten	a mango.	?

Will	Raj	have	sent	a letter	?
Will	Raj and Meena	have	written	a poem	?

Practice 4.9 A

Fill in the blanks with correct form the verbs into the correct form to make sentences of future perfect tense.

1. By 7o'clock they (finish) their work.
2. The studetns (leave) classroom by the end of the hour.
3. I(go)home by next month.
4. He (return) from the picnic by 7 p.m.
5. He (sell) his car by next week.
6. She (finish) shopping by 8p.m.
7. By the end of this month I (live) in this village for five years.
8. By evening Raj (complete) the painting work.
9. By 30th March they (study) in this school for 5 years.
10. They (play) fifty matches till the end of this year.

Practice 4.9 B

Fill in the blanks with suitable form of verbs to indicate future perfect tense.The first one has been done for you.

1. By the time she …………… (come back) home, she ………… .(finish) five years in U.A.E.
Answer: By the time she **comes back** home , she **will have finished** five years in U.A.E..
2. He …………….. (paint)the wall before his mother ………….(arrive)
3. They …….. (eat) a lot before the ice cream ……………(arrive).
4. The maid ………… (chop) the vegetables by the time Mrs.Hall…………..(enter) the house.
5. We ………… (fix) an appointment before the candidate ……… (call)

187

6. She .... (wash) all the clothes before she..........(leave) the home.

7. By the time Ravi............ (open) the door they ....(wait)for ten minutes.

8. You .... (study) in Delhi University for six years by the time you ....(get) a master's degree.

9. The postman .... (deliver) all the letters by 12 a.m.

10. He .... (pack) all the things when they ....(come) to take him with them.

Practice 4.9 C

Change the given sentences into negative and interrogative. The first one has been done for you.

1. I **shall have** opened the shop till 10.00 am.

Negative : I **shall not have** opened the shop till 10.00 am.

Interrogative: Shall I **have** opened the shop till 10.00 am?

2. We shall have seen the Taj till next Saturday.

Negative :..

Interrogative:..

3. You will have completed four years of service till next December.

Negative :..

Interrogative:..

4. They will have travelled in 7 countries till 15th March.

Negative :..

Interrogative:..

5. She will have washed all the clothes till 5 p.m.

Negative :..

Interrogative:..

6. He will have revised all the lessons till tomorrow morning.

Negative :..

Interrogative:..

7. Ajay will have seen all the photos by 5 p.m.

Negative :..

Interrogative:...

     8. The factory will have produced one million cars by 2025.

Negative :..

Interrogative:...

     9. The children will have learnt all alphabets till the end of the
year.

Negative :..

Interrogative:...

     10. The news will have reached to all the people by the end of the
day.

Negative :..

Interrogative:...

4.10 Present Perfect Continuous Tense

Let us read the story first:

Ravi **has been watching** cartoon show on TV since he was six years old. He likes to watch Cartoon shows. He plays cricket with other kids. He also goes for cycling with his friends.

Lately, he **has been drawing** some pictures in the drawing copy. He **has been showing** his drawings to his friends. He **has been telling** them what he would draw next.

Neelesh is Ravi's friend. Recently **he has been watching** cartoon shows with Ravi. He **has been wishing** to watch the cartoon shows for many years. But there was no television in his house. Now he can watch TV in Ravi's house.

This tense is used to speak about an action that recently stopped or is still going on. It tells about a finished action that influences the present.

Hints- all day, for 3 years, since 2005, how long, the whole week.

Structure: Subject+ have been/ has been+ ing form of the verb+ object+ since/for + time

Subject	Has been/ have been	Verb+ing	Object	Since/ for	Time/period	
I	have been	watching	a match	for	two hours.	.
we	have been	living	here	since	2008.	.
You	have been	coming	here	for	two weeks.	.
They	have been	writing	answers	for	two hours.	.
Raj and Teena	have been	playing	polo	for	half an hour.	.
He	has been	watching	a film	for	two hours.	.
She	has been	washing	clothes	since	ten o'clock.	.
It	has been	raining	heavily	since	morning.	.
Mohan	has been	writing	a letter	for	ten minutes.	.
Seema	has been	sending	letters	for	3 weeks.	.

| A dog | has been | barking | there | since | two o'clock. | . |
| A man | has been | standing | on the road | for | ten minutes. | . |

Negative Sentences:

Structure: Subject+ have not been/ has not been+ ing form of the verb+ object+ since/for + time.

Subject	Has not been/ have not been	Verb+ing	Object	Since/ for	Time/period	
I	have not been	watching	a match	for	two hours.	.
we	have not been	living	here	since	2008.	.
You	have not been	coming	here	for	two weeks.	.
They	have not been	writing	answers	for	two hours.	.
Raj and Teena	have not been	playing	polo	for	half an hour.	.
He	has not been	watching	a film	for	two hours.	.
She	has not been	washing	clothes	since	ten o'clock.	.
It	has not been	raining	heavily	since	morning.	.
Mohan	has not been	writing	a letter	for	ten minutes.	.

Interrogative Sentences:

Structure: Has/Have + Subject+ been+ ing form of the verb+ object+ since/for + time + ?

Have/ Has	Subject	been	Verb+ing	Object	Since/ for	Time/period	?
Have	I	been	watching	a match	for	two hours.	?
Have	we	been	living	here	since	2008.	?
Have	you	been	coming	here	for	two weeks.	?
Have	they	been	writing	answers	for	two hours.	?
Have	Raj and	been	playing	chess	for	half an hour.	?

	Ria						
Has	he	been	watching	a film	for	two hours.	?
Has	she	been	washing	clothes	since	ten o'clock.	?
Has	it	been	raining	heavily	since	morning.	?
Has	Raj	been	writing	a letter	for	ten minutes.	?

Uses of since and for in perfect continuous tense

Since	For		Since	For
definite point of time	period of time		definite point of time	period of time
morning	2 days		July	5 decades
evening	3 hours		Saturday	3 centuries
afternoon	15 minutes		2015	30 seconds
5 o'clock	3 weeks		last night	half an hour
9 p.m.	4 months		last century	ten years

Practice 4.10 A

Make sentences of present perfect continuous tense by using the verb given.

1. He/play in the ground for two hours.
2. You/watch TV all day.
3. I /wait for you for one week.
4. She/live in New Delhi for 2 years.
5. It/rain since afternoon.
6. We/ learn French for six months.
7. They /play cricket for 3 hours.
8. You /paint ceiling since morning.
9. Raj /travel by bus for 2 years.
10. Amita /write stories since her childhood.

Practice 4.10 B

Fill in the blanks with suitable form of verbs to make sentences of present continuous tense.

1. I .... (not/ complete) assignment yet.
2. It............. (rain) for about two hours.
3. Amit .... (be) at the cabin since 10 a.m.
4. We .... (play) cricket for 3 hours.
5. You............ (sit) in the park for 30 minutes.
6. The children...........(play) in the ground.
7. The driver ....(drive) a car.
8. The birds............(fly) in the sky.

Practice 4.10C

Change these sentences into negative and interrogative sentences .The first one has been done for you.
1. Ravi **has been watching** cartoon show on TV since he was six years old.

Negative : Ravi has not been watching cartoon show on TV since he was six years old.
Interrogative : Has Ravi not been watching cartoon show on TV since he was six years old?

2.He **has been drawing** some pictures in the drawing copy.
Negative : ....
Interrogative: ....
3.He **has been showing** his drawings to his friends.
Negative : ....
Interrogative: ....
4. He **has been telling** them what he would draw next.
Negative : ....
Interrogative: ....
5. Recently **he has been watching** cartoon shows with Ravi.
Negative : ....
Interrogative: ....
6. He **has been wishing** to watch the cartoon shows for many years.
Negative : ....

Interrogative: ....

4.11 Past perfect Continuous Tense

Let us read this story:

The players from other schools **had been arriving** in the school all morning before the cluster level games started. They saw the school building thoroughly. They liked the assembly hall the most. They also went to see the play ground.

The players were tired because they **had been traveling** for many hours. Before going to take rest they were curious to meet the members of other teams. They **had been introducing** themselves with other team members.

All the participants **had been practicing** for cluster level games for three months. Their coaches **had been training** them for competition. They **had been taking** special diet like banana and sprouts. The coach **had been selecting** the finest players to take part in competition.

This tense is used to speak about an action taking place before a certain time in past.

Hints- for, since, the whole day, all day

Structure: Subject + had been+ ing form of the verb+ object + since/ for + time.

Examples :

I had been studying for many years before getting my job.
They had been walking all day to reach the waterfall in the forest.
You had been sending messages for four months before coming here.

subject	had been	verb+ing	object	since/ for	time/period	
I	had been	watching	a match	for	two hours.	
we	had been	living	here	since	2008.	.
You	had been	coming	here	for	two weeks.	.
They	had been	writing	answers	for	two hours.	.
Raj and Ria	had been	playing	polo	for	half an hour.	.
He	had been	watching	a film	for	two hours.	.

She	had been	washing	clothes	since	ten o'clock.	.
It	had been	raining	heavily	since	morning.	.
Mohan	had been	writing	a letter	for	ten minutes.	.
Seema	had been	sending	letters	for	3 weeks.	.
A dog	had been	barking	there	since	two o'clock.	.

Negative Sentences:
Structure: Subject + had not been+ <u>ing form of the verb</u>+ object + since/ for + time.

subject	had not been	verb+ing	object	since/ for	time/period	.
I	had not been	watching	a match	for	two hours.	.
we	had not been	living	here	since	2008.	
You	had not been	coming	here	for	two weeks.	.
They	had not been	writing	answers	for	two hours.	.
Raj and Ria	had not been	playing	polo	for	half an hour.	.
He	had not been	watching	a film	for	two hours.	.
She	had not been	washing	clothes	since	ten o'clock.	.
It	had not been	raining	heavily	since	morning.	.
Mohan	had not been	writing	a letter	for	ten minutes.	.
Seema	had not been	sending	letters	for	3 weeks.	.
A dog	had not been	barking	there	since	two o'clock.	.

Interrogative Sentences:

Structure: Had+ Subject+ been+ ing form of the verb+ object + since/ for + time+?

Had	subject	been	verb+ing	object	since/ for	time/period	?
Had	I	been	watching	a match	for	two hours.	?
Had	we	been	living	here	since	2008.	?
Had	you	been	coming	here	for	two weeks.	?
Had	they	been	writing	answers	for	two hours.	?
Had	Raj and Ria	been	playing	polo	for	half an hour.	?
Had	he	been	watching	a film	for	two hours.	?
Had	she	been	washing	clothes	since	ten o'clock.	?
Had	it	been	raining	heavily	since	morning.	?
Had	Mohan	been	writing	a letter	for	ten minutes.	?
Had	Seema	been	sending	letters	for	3 weeks.	?
Had	a dog	been	barking	there	since	two o'clock.	?

Practice 4.11 A

Fill in the blank with suitable form of verb to make sentences of past perfect continuous tense.

1. We ………………..…cricket all the morning. (to play)
2. She ………………..…TV for two hours. (to watch)
3. He ………………..…ceiling all afternoon. (to paint)
4. They………………...…the answers throughout the evening. (to revise)
5. You …………………... in that school for four years.(to teach)
6. Rajiv …………………...for you for three months.(to wait)
7. I ………………..……… by train to reach my office.(to travel)
8. Deepa ………..…………stamps for ten years.(to collect)
9. The children …………the swing for many years. (to use)

10. The Election Commission …………..fair elections since its establishment.(to organize)

Practice 4.11 B

Change these sentences into negative and interrogative sentences .The first one has been done for you.

1. The players from other schools **had been arriving** in the school all the morning before the cluster level games started.

Negative   : The players **had not been arriving** in the school all the afternoon.

Interrogative : **Had** the players **been arriving** in the school all the afternoon?

2. They had been traveling for many hours.

Negative   : ………………………………………………

Interrogative : ………………………………………………

3. They **had been introducing** themselves with other team members.

Negative   : ………………………………………………

Interrogative : ………………………………………………

4.All the participants **had been practicing** for cluster level games for three months.

Negative   : ………………………………………………

Interrogative : ………………………………………………

5.Their coaches **had been training** them for competition.

Negative   : ………………………………………………

Interrogative : ………………………………………………

6.They **had been taking** special diet like banana and sprouts.

Negative   : ………………………………………………

Interrogative : ………………………………………………

7.Each coach **had been selecting** the finest players to take part in competition.

Negative   : ………………………………………………

Interrogative : ………………………………………………

4.12 Future Perfect Continuous Tense

Let us read the story first:

Deepak is a tourist. He has been travelling to various countries for many years. This January, he **will have been completing** visiting 16 countries. He **will have been traveling** for 8 years.

This year Deepak has planned to go to France. In March, he is going to Paris. He **will have been touring** to a European country for 4 years. He will stay in hotel of Golden Lion Brand. He will be staying in such a hotel for fourth time.

Next year he will marry Rose .He **will have been planning** to travel with her .Rose **will have been getting** a unique experience in her life. She **will have been enjoying** the best kind of marriage life full of traveling and tourism.

We use the future perfect continuous tense to show that something will continue up until a particular event or time in the future. Here we Put emphasis on the course of an action.

Hints- for, the last couple of hours, all day long

Structure: subject + shall have been/ will have been + ing form of the verb+ object+ since/for + time

Example-They will have been talking for over an hour by the time Dinesh arrives.

Subject	shall have been/will have been	verb+ing	object	since/ for	time/period
I	shall have been	watching	a match	for	two hours.
we	shall have been	living	here	since	2015.
You	will have been	coming	here	for	two weeks.
They	will have been	writing	answers	for	two hours.
Raj and Sue	will have been	playing	polo	for	half an hour.
He	will have been	watching	a film	for	two hours.
She	will have been	washing	clothes	since	ten o'clock.
It	will have been	raining	heavily	since	morning.
Mohan	will have been	writing	a letter	for	ten minutes.
Seema	will have been	sending	letters	for	3 weeks.

Negative Sentences:

Structure: subject + shall not have been/ will not have been + ing form of the verb+ object+ since/for + time+punctuation mark.

Subject	shall not have been/will not have been	verb+ing	object	since/ for	time/period
I	shall not have been	watching	a match	for	two hours.
we	shall not have been	living	here	since	2015.
You	will not have been	coming	here	for	two weeks.
They	will not have been	writing	answers	for	two hours.
Raj and Sue	will not have been	playing	polo	for	half an hour.
He	will not have been	watching	a film	for	two hours.
She	will not have been	washing	clothes	since	ten o'clock.
It	will not have been	raining	heavily	since	morning.

Mohan	will not have been	writing	a letter	for	ten minutes.
Seema	will not have been	sending	letters	for	3 weeks.

Interrogative Sentences:

Structure: Shall/Will +S + have been + ing form of the verb+ object+ since/for + time?

Will/ Shall	Subject	have been	verb+ing	object	since/ for	time/period	?
Shall	I	have been	watching	a match	for	two hours.	?
Shall	we	have been	living	here	since	2015.	?
Will	you	have been	coming	here	for	two weeks.	?
Shall	they	have been	writing	answers	for	two hours.	?
Shall	Raj and Sue	have been	playing	chess	for	half an hour.	?
Shall	he	have been	watching	a film	for	two hours.	?
Shall	she	have been	washing	clothes	since	ten o'clock.	?
Shall	it	have been	raining	heavily	since	morning.	?
Shall	Mohan	have been	writing	a letter	for	ten min.	?
Shall	Seema	have been	sending	letters	for	3 weeks.	?

Practice 4.12 A

Fill in the blanks with suitable form of verbs to make sentences of future perfect continuous tense.

1. By the end of the year we..................... (study) English for 6 years.
2. By the end of the week I .... (live) in this house for three months.
3. By the end of this month he .... (work) as a driver for two years.
4. You ....…......... .(look) for a job for three months by next Monday.
5. By 6 p.m. she .... (read) a novel for three hours.
6. The staff members .... (wait) for the chief guest for fifty minutes.
7. She ....…......... (cook) in the kitchen for one hour.
8. The children .... (play) in the ground since morning.

201

9. The passengers .... (buy) tickets from the counter.

10. By 8o'clock I .... (watch) TV for two hours.

Practice 4.12B

Change these sentences into negative and interrogative sentences .The first one has been done for you.

1. This January, he **will have been completing** visiting 16 countries.

Negative   : This January he will not have been competing visiting 16 countries.

Interrogative: Will he be completing visiting 16 countries this January?

2. He will have been traveling for 8 years.

Negative   : ....

Interrogative: ....

3.He will have been touring to a European country for 4 years.

Negative   : ....

Interrogative: ....

4.He will be staying in such a hotel for fourth time.

Negative   : ....

Interrogative: ....

5.He will have been planning to travel with her .

Negative   : ....

Interrogative: ....

6. Rose will have been getting a unique experience in her life.

Negative   : ....

Interrogative: ....

7. She will have been enjoying the best kind of marriage life full of traveling and tourism.

Negative   : ....

Interrogative: ....

Answers:

Practice 4.1A: 1. takes 2.works 3.thank 4.hopes 5.try
Practice 4.1 B (i) contains (ii) buy (iii) reaches (iv) carry (v) fixes (vi) gets (vii) wait (viii) cries (ix) grazes
Practice 4.1C (i) spends (ii) gets (iii) play (iv) reads (v) tell (vi) sets (vii) brings (viii) wash
Practice 4.1 D:
1. Does he want to have a lemon juice?
2. Do the children like cookies?
3.Does the teacher bring a duster?
4.Does she guide the passengers?
5.Does the train come late everyday?
Practice4.1 E
1. Does 2.Do 3.Does 4.Do 5. Do 6. Does 7.Does 8.Does 9.Does 10. Does

Practice4.1 F
1. I don't believe in his story.
2. The officers did not attend the meeting in the hall.
3. The shopkeeper does not open the shop early.
4. This toy does not work well.
5. His car does not move smoothly .
6. You father does not work in an office.
7 .His kite does fly high.
8.He does not open this shop early.

Practice 4.2 A:
1. He forgot his umbrella.
2. They listened this news with shock
3. Ruby caught the morning train.
4. Michael liked the idea.
5. The newspaper described the city in detail.
Practice: 4.2 B
1.Wrote 2.Took 3. Helped 4.arrived 5.flew 6. gave 7.sold 8 cancelled 9.washed 10. opened

Practice: 4.2 C
1. He did not complete his homework in the evening.
2. The government did not propose a new tax.
3. Rajkumar did not wash a shirt.
4. You did not attend the lecture of Mr.Johnson.
5. The birds did not fly away.
6. The kite did not reach high.

5. Passive voice

There are two different ways of presenting the same thing.

I take tea.
Tea is taken be me.

In the first sentence, the subject performs the action whereas in the second sentence, the subject of the verb is acted upon. It means the subject of the first sentence becomes the object of the verb of the second sentence.

See the difference in the sentences of both the columns in the table:

I take tea	Tea is taken by me.
We play cricket.	Cricket is played by us.
They call me.	I am called by them.
He has closed the door.	The door has been closed by him.
She has seen the film.	The film has been seen by her.

Raj will tell a story.	A story will be told by Raj.
You are reading a newspaper.	A news paper is being read by you.

In order to understand the difference between active and passive voice the following two paragraphs are given.

Preparation of Independence Day: Active Voice

The school will celebrate Independence Day tomorrow. The students have decorated the school campus. The workers are arranging chairs. The physical education teacher has trained the students for March Past. The senior students have decorated the stage very nicely. The programme will start at 7.00 A.M. The principal will unfurl the national flag. He will observe the march past. The students will sing National Anthem. The girls of class XI will perform a dance. Some students will deliver speeches. The Principal has invited the respected people of the city. He has invited News Reporters also. The Principal will give awards to the toppers of previous year. The top two position holders of the march past will also receive trophies. Sweets will be distributed at the end of the celebration.

Independence Day Report: Passive Voice

Independence Day was celebrated in the school yesterday. The school campus has been decorated by the students. Chairs were being arranged by workers. The students had been trained by the physical education teacher for March Past. The stage had been decorated by the senior students very nicely. The programme was started at 7.00 A.M. The National Flag was unfurled by the Principal. The March Past was observed by him. The National Anthem was sung by the students. A dance was performed by girls of class XI. Speeches were delivered by some students. The respected people of the city were invited by the Principal. Some News reporters were also invited. The awards were given away by the Principal to the toppers of the previous year. Trophies were given to the top two position holders of the march past. In the end of the celebration sweets were distributed.

[The table below tells the structure of passive voice in various tenses. To emphasize that 'object' of a sentence of active voice become 'subject' in passive voice and vice versa, the structures of passive voices are written in such a way that the word 'Object' is written in the beginning and 'Subject' is written in the end after 'by']

Present simple active S+ v+ s/es + o	present simple passive O+ is/am/are+ v3 + by +subject
Example- I take tea. You buy a book. We sing a song. They carry a bag. He writes a letter.	Example - Tea is taken by me. A book is bought by you. A song is sung by us. A bag is carried by them. A letter is written by him.
Past simple passive S+ v2 + object	past simple passive Object + was/were+ v3 + by +subject
I took tea. You bought two books. We sang a song. They carried a bag. He wrote a letter.	Tea was taken by me. Two books were bought by you. A song was sung by us. A bag was carried by them. A letter was written by him.
Future simple [active voice] s+ will/shall + object	future simple [passive voice] object + will be/shall be + v3 + by + subject
I shall take tea. You will buy a book. He shall call me. They will carry a bag. He will write a letter.	Tea will be taken by me. A book will be bought by you. I shall be called by him. A bag will be carried by them. A letter will be written by him

present continuous tense (active voice) S+ is/am/are+ v+ ing + object I am taking tea. You are buying 5 books. We are singing a song. They are carrying a bag. He is calling me.	**present continuous tense (passive voice)** object+ is/am/are+ being+v3+by + subject Tea is being taken by me. Five books are being bought by you. A song is being sung by us. A bag s being carried by them. I am being called by him.
past continuous tense (active voice) s+was/were+ v+ing + object I was taking tea. You were buying 5 books. We were singing a song. They were carrying a bag. He was calling me.	**past continuous tense (passive voice)** object+ was/were+ being+v3+by + subject Tea was being taken by me. 5 books were being bought by you. A song was being sung by us. A bag was being carried by them. I was being called by him.
Present Perfect tense [Active Voice] [s+has/have+v3+object] I have taken tea. You have bought 5 books. We have sung a song. They have carried a bag. He has called me.	**Present Perfect tense [Passive Voice]** [object+ has been/have been+v3+by subject] Tea has been taken by me. 5 books have been bought by you. A song has been sung by us. A bag has been carried by them. I have been called by him.
past perfect tense [Active Voice] [s+had+v3+object] I had taken tea. You had bought 5 books. We had sung a song.	**past perfect tense [Passive Voice]** [s+had been+v3+by+object] Tea had been taken by me. 5 books had been bought by you. A song had been sung by us.

They had carried a bag. He had called me.	A bag had been carried by them. I had been called by him.
future perfect tense [Active Voice] **[s+ will have/shall have+v3+object]** I will have taken tea. You will have bought 5 books. We will have sung a song. They will have carried a bag. He will have called me.	**future perfect tense [Passive Voice]** **[s+ will have been/shall have been +v3+by + object]** Tea will have been taken by me. 5 books will have been bought by you. A song will have been sung by us. A bag will have been carried by them. I shall have been called by him.

The voice indicates whether subject performs the action or the subject receives the action.

Active Voice-When the subject of the verb acts, the verb is said to be in Active voice.

Passive Voice- When the subject of the verb receives the action, the verb is said to be in passive voice.

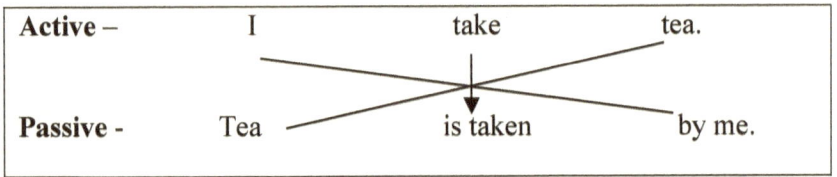

 We can change a sentence of active voice in a sentence of passive voice by following certain steps. These steps are given here:

1. **Change the subject-** The subject of the Active Voice becomes the object of the Passive Voice.

> **Active** : Ram likes mangoes

> **Passive**: Mangoes are liked by Ram.

2. **Change the object-** The Object of the Active Voice becomes the subject of the Passive Voice.

> **Active:** Mary sings a song.
>
> **Passive:** A song is sung by Mary.

3. **Form of 'Be'** is added in Passive Voice.

Form of 'Be'--- is, am, are-------------Present Tense **was ,were ---------- -Past Tense** **being ---------------- --Continuous Tense** **been --------------------Perfect Tense**

Example-

> **Active Voice-** He plays hockey. [Present indefinite tense]
> **Passive voice-** Hockey **is** played by him.

> **Active Voice-** He sent a letter. [Past indefinite tense]
> **Passive voice-** A letter **was** sent by him.

> **Active Voice-** They are singing a song. [Present continuous]
> **Passive voice-** A song **is being** sung by them.

> **Active Voice-**She has written a letter. [Present Perfect Tense]
> **Passive voice-** A letter **has been** written by her.

4. **'by'** is added before the object of the Passive Voice.

> **Active Voice:** They watch a movie.
> **Passive Voice:** A movie is watched by them.

5.   Pronouns are changed in the following way:

Pronoun	Changed into
I	me
we	us
you	you
they	them
He	him
She	her
It	it

In the same way if the object in Active voice is 'her', it will change into subject 'she' in passive voice.

For example-

Active Voice- I called him.
Passive Voice- He was called by me.
Active Voice- They taught me.
Passive Voice- I was taught by them.
Active Voice- You called us.
Passive Voice- We were called by you.

6. Past Participle form of the verb is used after the form of 'be'

Example-

Active Voice: He **takes** tea
Passive Voice: Tea is **taken** by him.
Active Voice: Raj **helps** me.
Passive Voice: I am **helped** by Raj.

7. Tense of the verb remains the same. Only its form is changed.

Active Voice- I called him.   [Past simple tense]

Passive Voice- He was called by me.   [Past simple tense]

8. Vague subjects like someone, somebody, everybody, everyone; people etc. are dropped in Passive Voice form-

Active Voice- Someone opened the door.
Passive Voice-The door was opened.

Active Voice- Somebody is calling my name.
Passive Voice- My name is being called.
9. Passive voice of interrogative sentences.
Active : Do you like oranges?
Passive : Are oranges liked by you?

First we have to identify the tense of the sentence. In the sentence given above we see that helping verb 'Do' is used. It means that this sentence is of present simple tense. Now we change it into passive voice. As in the present simple tense helping verb is/am/are are used in passive voice we have to select the right helping verb. The subject 'oranges' is plural so we have to use helping verb 'are' in the passive voice. In the interrogative sentences helping verb comes before the subject so we write 'Are' before the subject 'oranges' and complete the sentence by adding third form of main verb, by and object .
More examples-
    Did he help you?
    Were you helped by him?
    Was Radha playing cricket?
    Was cricket being played by Radha?
    Have you asked a question?
    Has a question been asked by you?
    Will she like this photo?
    Will this photo be liked by her?
10. Passive voice of negative sentences-
    Active voice: I do not like oranges.

Passive voice: Oranges are not liked by me.

It is clear that to make passive voice of a negative sentence not is adding after the helping verb (to be verb).

Active: He did not open the door.
Passive: The door was not opened by him.
Active: Have you called the nurse?
Passive: Has the nurse been called by you?
Active: Will they like this idea?
Passive: Will this idea be liked by them?
Active: Raj does not buy cherries.
Passive: cherries are not bought by Raj.
Active: Don't open the door.
Passive : Let the door not be opened.
Active: She is not taking music lessons.
Passive: Music lessons are not being taken by her.

In sentence which have '**not….any**' construction, the structure in passive voice changes a little.

Active: I am not taking any medicine.
Passive: No medicine is being taken by me.
Active: They have not kept any precaution.
Passive: No precaution has been kept by them.

11A. Passive Voice of Modal Auxiliaries would, should, may, can, could, must, ought to – To change into passive voice modal is followed by 'be' and then third form of the verb is written. Others rules remain the same.

can make--------------------can be made

May make--------------------may be made

Should call-------------------should be called

Active voice	Passive voice
She might take tea.	Tea might be taken by her.
I would write a letter.	A letter would be written by me.
He should decide the route.	The route should be decided by him.
They ought to change the subject.	The subject ought to be changed by them.
Thomas need not mix milk.	Milk need not be mixed by Thomas.
The manager would open the lock.	The lock would be opened by the manager.
The company could make the policy.	The policy could be made by the company.

11B. Passive voice of might have, can have, could have, should have etc-

Might have, could have, should have etc. change into might have been, could have been and should have been respectively.

He could have played cricket.	Cricket could have been played by him.
They should have taken tea.	Tea should have been taken by them.
She might have won the match.	The match might have been won by her.
We must have bought the ticket.	The ticket must have been bought by us.

12. Changing **imperative sentence [Commands, orders, advice etc.]** into passive voice-

Clean this window.
Go out of the room.
Please help me to solve this problem
Let her enjoy her party.

In these sentences subject is hidden. That subject 'you' is understood. We can change into passive voice in the following three ways-

A] Let + object+ be/not be+ third form of the verb

Clean this window.	Let this window be cleaned.
Do that.	Let that be done.
Let them enjoy the party.	Let the party be enjoyed by them.
Open the door.	Let the door be opened.

B] Command, request, order or advice is changed into passive voice by beginning the sentence as- You are commanded, You are requested, You are ordered, You are advised etc.

Kindly go through this letter.	You are requested to go through this letter.
Work sincerely.	You are advised to work sincerely.
Stand up outside.	You are ordered to stand up outside.
Please help me to open the door.	You are requested to help me to open the door.

13. Changing **infinitive verbs** into passive voice.

To+verb is changed into to be +third form of the verb

active voice	passive voice
to + verb	to be+ third form of the verb

Examples-

1. **Active Voice** – He worked hard to pass the exam.
Passive Voice- He worked hard for the exam to be passed.
2. **Active Voice-** It is time to close the shop.
Passive Voice- It is time for the shop to be closed.
3. **Active Voice-** We decided to make him captain.
Passive Voice- He was decided to be made captain by us.
4. **Active Voice-** Children like elders to gift them.
Passive voice- Children like to be gifted by elders.
5. **Active Voice-** It is necessary to take the medicine.
Passive Voice- It is necessary for the medicine to be taken.

14. Two objects of the verb- When a subject has two objects then it is easier to make the object near the verb to be made subject. However both the objects can be made subject.

When first and second object refer to the same person or thing then passive voice will be made in only one way. [See example 3]

Example 1

Active-   They gave **us(1) this toy(2)**.

   Passive-   **We** were given this toy by them.
                        [First object is made subject]
                  Or
            This toy was given to us by them.
                        [Second object is made subject]

Example 2

Active   I shall teach   **him (1) English (2).**

Passive-   **He** will be taught English by me.
                        [First object is made subject]
                        or

English will be taught to him by me.

[Second object is made subject]

Example 3

Active: We elected **him** (1) **President (2)**.
 Passive-   **He** was elected President by us.

[Since both the first and second objects refer to the same person so the object close to the verb is made the subject in passive voice.]

15. Prepositional sentences-

If any preposition is used with verb then in the passive voice too, the same preposition is used.

Examples-

Active Voice-- I was speaking to him.
Passive Voice--He was being spoken to by me.

Active-Ram looked at the picture.
Passive -The picture was looked at by Ram.

Active --She agreed to the decision.
Passive --The decision was agreed to by her.

Active ---You must look after your younger brother.
Passive --Your younger brother must be looked after by you.

16 .Passive voice without the agent

When we have to give more emphasis to action in comparison to the doer of the action then object/agent (doer of the action) is not used.

Example-

Active Voice	Passive Voice
We ought to respect our teachers.	Our teachers must be respected.
We saw you take the toy.	You were seen to take the toy.

Everyone should pay taxes in time.	Taxes should be paid in time.
Someone should show me the way.	I should be showed the way.
People elected him President.	He was elected President.

17. When 'by' is not used in passive voice-

While making passive of following verbs 'by' is not used .In place of 'by' a suitable preposition is used.

Know, annoy, alarm, contain, displease, please, line, marry, offend, surprise, satisfy, charge, shock, interest, throng, disgust

Active Voice	Passive Voice
His words offended me.	I was offended at his words.
He knows me.	I am known to him.
Her behavior annoys me.	I am annoyed at her behavior.
Krishna married Rukmani.	Rukmani was married to Krishna.
Your work satisfies me.	I am satisfied with you work.
We cannot please you.	You cannot be pleased with us.
This box contains files.	The files are contained in this box.
The students lined the gallery.	The gallery was lined with students.
Sit down	Be seated.
You should keep your promise.	Your promise should be kept.

18. When 'to' is used in passive voice.

In some verbs preposition 'to' is not used in active voice.

Example- I made them **write.**

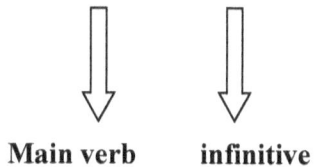

Main verb   infinitive

While changing it in passive voice 'to' is added after main verb and before the infinitive.

Passive- They were made **to** write.

Active voice	Passive voice
We heard the boys shout.	The boys were heard to shout.
I watched him bringing water.	He was watched to bring water.
My mother made me buy the ticket.	I was made to buy the ticket by my mother.
She let me come.	I was let to go.

19. Miscellaneous sentences-

Active voice	Passive voice
May I go out?	Am I allowed to go out?
One should keep one's promise.	Promise should be kept.
They say that you are a thief.	It is said that you are a thief.
One cannot help it.	It cannot be helped.
God helps those who help themselves.	Those who are helped by themselves are helped by God.
People say that honesty is the best policy.	It is said that honesty is the best policy.
The rose smells sweet.	The rose is sweet when smelt.

20. No passive for intransitive verb.

The following verbs come in the category of intransitive verbs. It means these verbs have no object .So there is no passive voice for these verbs.

> agree, appear, arrive, belong, collapse, come, consist of ,depend, die, disappear, exist, fall, go ,inquire, lie, live ,look, occur, remain, respond, sit, sleep, stand, swim, vanish, wake

Practice 1

Change into passive voice-

1. I like Vanilla ice-creams.
2. The leader tossed the coin.
3. They have received the orders.

4. I pulled the door.
5. She attended the morning class.
6. The monkey plucked the mango.

Practice 2

Change into passive voice-

1. Did he attend the class?
2. Did Mr. Sharma identify you?
3. Shall we get new copies today?

4. Will you buy books this year?
5. Have you taken tea?
6. Has Raj opened the lock?

Answers:((Practice 1)

1. Vanilla ice-creams are liked by me.
2. The coin was tossed by the leader.
3. The orders have been received by them.
4. The door was pulled by me.

5. The morning class was attended by her.
6. The mango was plucked by the monkey.

Answers (Practice 2)

1. Was the class attended by him?
2. Were you identified by Mr.Sharma?
3. Will new copies be got by us today?

4. Will books be bought by you this year?
5. Has tea been taken by you ?
6. Has the lock been opened by Raj?

6. Modal Verbs

A verb such as may, can or will that is used with another verb (not a modal) to express possibility, permission, intention etc. are called modal verbs or modal auxiliaries.

Modal verbs have only one form. They have no –ing or -ed forms and do not add –s to the third person singular form.
- He can speak English.
- They will visit tomorrow.
- John may reach at 5 pm.
- She must be ready till 2o'clock.

The modal verbs are can, could, may ,might, must, ought to ,shall ,will and would.

Dare, need, have to and used to also share some of the features of modal verbs.

Questions are formed without do/does in the present, or did in the past.

- Can I invite Reeta?
- Should I inform them?
- Might it rain today?

Negative sentences are formed with not or the short form –n't and do not use do/does or did.

Can and could-
1. 'Can' and 'could' are used to say that someone is able to do something. Could is simple past tense of can.

- He can compose really good songs.
- Can you help me?
- Raj can run faster than John.
- She could already count up to ten before she started school.
- He ran as fast as he could.

2. 'Can' and 'could' may also be used to say that someone is allowed to do something.

- My father says I can't go to school on my own.
- My mother says you can come to our house for lunch.
- He can't go inside without a ticket.

3. Can and could are also used for asking for information or help, for offering something, and for suggesting something.

- Can you tell me if this bus goes to Bhopal?
- Could you show me where the accident took place?
- You can borrow my book, if you like.
- You could take help of your brother.
- Your brother can join us, if he wishes to.
- She can come by evening train.

Will and would-
1. Will and would are used when we ask someone to do something.
- Will you please stop talking?
- Would you give me that book please?
- Please, Will you close the window?
- Will you lend me your pen please?

2. We can also use will and would to offer something or to suggest something.
- Will I carry this bag to the station?
- Would you like another drink?
- Which book would you like?
- Wouldn't it be better to stay and wait?

Shall and should –
We use shall and should to ask for advice, offer something and suggest something.
- Should I bring my clothes with me?
- Should I close the door?
- Shall we go now?
- Shall I catch the train, or will it be better to hire a taxi?
- Shall I help you with that suitcase?
- You should try this new mobile phone.

Ought to–
'Ought to' is used to make strong suggestions and talk about someone's duty.

- You look tired. You ought to take rest now.
- I ought to eat more nutritious food.
- We ought to lock the door before leaving the shop.
- You ought to switch off the light when you are going out of the room.
- She ought to know how to use a computer.
- The students ought to maintain silence in the classroom.

Must-

We use 'must' to talk about things that we have to do. In the past tense too 'must' has the same form. The contraction of must not is 'mustn't.'

- I must post this letter now.
- You must take rest. You are very weak.
- Kids must not play with mobile phones.
- Why must I wash this floor today?
- They mustn't let their dog move on a busy road.

May and might-
1. One uses 'may' to ask if he is allowed to do something and to tell someone that he/she is allowed to do something.
- May I go out to watch a movie?
- May I borrow your copy?
- May you come with us to the market?
- Please may I see your admit card?
- Raj may leave now.
- You may not see that file.

2. 'May' and 'might' are used to talk about things that are possible or likely.
- Take a raincoat. It may rain.
- We might visit this zoo again.
- You may not have money to buy that car.
- If you are not watchful, you may fall.
- "Is he going to the market?" "I don't know. He might or he might not."

Practice 1

Fill in the gaps with the right modal. Use CAN'T or MUST.
1. You've been working all day long. You ……… be tired.
2. That lawyer….......... be pretty famous in the town. Everyone knows him.
3. That hotel ……… be very good. It is always empty.
4. The weather was stormy everyday during their holiday, so they …….. have had a very nice holiday.
5. Despite his wife's weakness, the baby was delivered safely. The couple …………be very happy and relieved.
6. He got here very quickly. He……. have taken a taxi.

Practice 2
Choose the best answer to explain these given situations.
1. The suitcase you bought is of very good quality.
a) It must have been very expensive.
b) It can't have been very expensive

2. My friend Mary walked past me without speaking.

a) She must have seen me.

b) She can't have seen me.

3. The phone rang but I didn't hear it.

a) I must have been asleep.

b) I can't have been asleep.

4. I haven't seen our neighbors for ages.

a) They must have gone away.

b) They can't have gone away.

5. I can't find my mobile phone.

a) I can't have left it in the restaurant we had dinner at last evening.

b) I must have left it in the restaurant we had dinner at last evening.

Practice 3

Choose the correct answer to fill in the blanks - must, mustn't & needn't.

1. This is a very precious ring. You .... lose it.

a) must b) mustn't c) needn't

2. She will be having lessons for another two hours. We .... visit him now.

a) must b) mustn't c) needn't

3. You .... wash those apples. They've already been washed.

a) must b) mustn't c) needn't

4. We .... hurry. We've got plenty of time.

a) must b) mustn't c) needn't

5. We have enough vegetables in the kitchen so we .... buy some more.

a) must b) mustn't c) needn't

6. This is a very great novel. You ...... read it.

a) must b) mustn't c) needn't

7. Time is not on our side. We ...... hurry.

a) must b) mustn't c) needn't

Practice 4 Fill in the gap with could, may, can, must, might, should.

1 .If he ......have solved the problem, he would have felt happier.

2. They ....work harder if they are to succeed.

3. You ....take an umbrella with you, in case it starts to rain.

4. I ....answer his letter as soon as possible.

5. He …..walk thirty miles a day.

6. When she was young she……….swim across the lake.

7. …………you please tell me how to get to M.G.street?

8. You …….try asking the bus driver to help you.

9. He wished he ……….visit Kashmir.

10. She ………..have caught the bus if she had left early.

11. I would be glad if I ………..help you.

12. …………I have some more coffee?

Answers:

Practice 1:1. must, 2.must,3.can't 4.can't, 5.must 6.must

Practice2: 1.a 2.b 3.a 4.a 5.b

Practice 3: 1 .b) mustn't 2.b) mustn't 3.c) needn't 4.c) needn't 5.c) needn't 6.a) must 7.a) must

Practice 4: 1 could, 2.must, 3 should, 4.must, 5.can, 6.could, 7.could, 8.may, 9.could, 10.might, 11.could, 12.may

7. Determiners

Determiner is a word that fixes or limits the meaning of a noun.

For example-

Dinesh is <u>my</u> friend.

I have <u>a</u> chocolate.

There is <u>little</u> water in the bottle.

This book is <u>yours</u>.

I have <u>some</u> pencils.

<u>Every</u> student should have a pen.

<u>That</u> bag is <u>yours</u>.

Kinds of Determiners

1. Possessive Determiners
2. Numerical Determiners
3. Quantitative Determiners
4. Demonstrative Determiners.
5. Article

1. Possessive determiner

The determiners which are used before nouns to show the idea of possession are called Possessive determiners. These determiners are possessive adjectives.

This is **my** book.
That is **your** home.
These are **our** benches.
His brother painted **his** home.
She washed **her** dress.
They sold **their** house.
That is **our** school.
He wants to use **his** laptop.

Practice 1

1 India is ……………country and I am proud of it.
2. "Mind………..business." the teacher ordered.
3. Do you help ………mother in cooking food?
4. They should improve …………writing skill.
5. That dog is biting …………..tail.

2. Numerical Determiner

The determiners which mention the number of a noun are called numerical determiners.

These are of two types-

1. Definite Numerical Determiner.

      i] **Cardinals:** one, two, three ….etc.

      ii] **Ordinals**: First, second, third ….etc.

2. Indefinite Numerical Determiner.

      i] **Many**- It means 'a large number of' (people/things etc.)

ii] **Few, a few, the few**- We use few, a few with plural countable nouns. 'Few' means 'not many' while a few means 'a small number'. 'The few' means the whole, whatever the particular number may be.

iii] **Some, any** [Some is used in affirmative sentences while any is used in the formation of negative and interrogative sentences. Some is used to indicate an unspecified number but it is a considerable number.]

iv] **Several**- it means more than two but not many.

v] **All**

Example- He has many friends.

A few people came to see the film.

There were few students in the book shop that day.

I wrote a few articles for magazines last year.

He has several pockets in his trousers.

3. Distributive Numeral Determiners-

i] **Each**-It means every one separately. It gives idea of one by one .It emphasizes individuality. It is used with two things.

ii] **Every**-It distributes a thing/attribute in a group in such a way that no member is left out. It is used for more than two things. It considers things or people in group together as one unit.

iii] **Neither** -not one and not the other

iv] **Either** (one or the other) - Either is used to make comparison between two ideas, when only one idea will come to pass. It offers a choice between two possibilities.

iv] **None**

Example:

I know each one of your group.

Every student will get a book.

Either of you may come here.

Either of us can do it.

He isn't ready to sing. We aren't either.

None of them was present.
Neither of his sisters was ready.
He had bags in each hand.
The trains are available every day.

Practice 2

1. ……..students are good at English. [a few/a little/any]
2. I have ….books on grammar.[some/any/the]
3. Have you ....book on grammar? [some /any/the]
4. How…………books do you need? [much/ many/ more]
5. Ram goes to temple ….. Sunday .[Each/Every/any]

3. Quantitative Determiner-

The determiners which mention the quantity of a noun are called Quantitative Determiners.

For example-

1] much- Much denotes quantity of a noun. It shows large amount.
- There is much water in the bucket.
- There is much salt in stock.
- Interrogative- How much is it?
- Negative-I don't have much money with me.

2] Little, a little, the little

'Little' means not much. It is a negative adjective. this amount indicated by 'little' is almost nothing.

'A little' means some at least. It is used to show a small amount that is enough.

'The little' means the whole, whatever the particular quantity may be.

Examples-I have little money. I can't afford travel this month.
I have a little sugar, enough for two cups of tea.

There was only a little oil left in the bottle.

They spent

3] Some, any

Some- Some is used with uncountable nouns or plural countable nouns to mean 'an amount of '. Some means a little when it is used in affirmative sense.

Some water, some time, some children, some books.

Any-It is used in negative and interrogative sense.

Are there any stamps?
I didn't eat any bread.
I have got hardly any money.
You can't go out without any shoes.
Do you have any questions?
Any place, any time, any place

Practice 3

Fill in the blanks with suitable quantitative determiner:

1. I can't lend you.........money.
2. I have ....money to spend on luxury.
3. Is there ....message for me?
4. There is .... water in the jug.
5. There is not ....flour in the tin.
6. Are there.......cassettes in this box?
7. Is there ....danger in hunting?
8. He has ....books in his library.

4. Demonstrative Determiner

The determiners which point out a thing, place or person are called demonstrative determiners. This, that, these and those are demonstrative determiners. This and that are used with singular noun. 'This' indicates nearby object/person. That indicates object and persons which are at some distance from the speaker. 'These' indicates plural nearby objects while 'those' is used with plural nouns which are situated at some distance.

Example:

This pen is mine.   That car is yours.

These books are yours.   Those bags are theirs.

5. Articles

Articles are of two categories .Definite and indefinite articles. [This topic is dealt in detail in the beginning of the book. Here a few exercises are given for practice.]

Practice 4

Fill in the blanks with appropriate article-
1. Mahesh is ...............M.A.
2. What............... Beautiful flower!
3..............Headmaster is on leave today.
4...................Earth is round.

Practice 5

1. He is ........M.L.A.
2. Ram bought ....ox from a fair.
3. What ....beautiful flower!
4............boy who is bowling is my brother.
5...........Headmaster is on leave today.

6. Mahesh is ……….one eyed person.

7. ………….person who came to see me today is my uncle.

8. ………….rich should help the poor.

9. Ram drives car sixty miles……….hour.

10. He is ………….best boy in the class.

Answers:

Practice 1: 1.my 2.your 3.your 4.their 5.its

Practice 2: 1. a few 2.some 3.any 4. Many 5.every

Practice 3: 1.any 2.no 3.any 4.some 5.any 6.any 7.any 8.many

Practice 4: 1. an 2 a 3.the 4.the

Practice 5: 1.an 2.an 3.a 4.The 5.The 6.a 7.The 8. The 9.an 10.the

8. Non finite verbs

Introduction-

Let us see these sentences:

- A boy plays cricket.(Singular sub + singular verb)

- Boys play cricket.   (plural sub + plural verb)

Here verbs are controlled by the number of their subject. Such verbs are called finite verbs.

Now see some more sentences-

- He is young.
- They are young.

- You are young.

Here finite verb forms agree with the subject in person and number.

Again-

Finite verb forms are marked for tense. For example-

- He is writing a letter now.
- He was writing a letter yesterday.

The contrast between the present tense and the past tense becomes obvious.

But, all the above three conditions do not apply to the non-finite verbs. The sentences given below illustrate this-

- I asked him <u>to obey</u> his parents.
- I like his <u>obeying</u> his parents.
- <u>Obeying</u> parents is a virtue.
- <u>Having obeyed</u> his parents, he left for the job.

Here the underlined verbs are not controlled by the number or person of their subject. These are non-finite verbs.

Now consider these two sentences-

- A boy likes <u>to play</u> cricket.
- Boys like <u>to play</u> cricket.

Here again the underlined verbs are not controlled by the number or person of their subject .These are non-finite verbs.

Definition- A verb that is not controlled by the number and person of its subject is called a *non-finite verb*.

The two verb forms beginning with 'to' and ending with '-ing' respectively are called Infinitive and Gerund. They are mutually exclusive .For example-

- <u>To laugh</u> is good for health.
- <u>Laughing</u> is good for health.

They can also act as object of a verb and preposition.

- I saw a <u>dancing</u> girl.
- He was a <u>tired</u> man.

The two verb forms ending with '-ing' and '-ed' respectively are called Present Participle and Past Participle. Present participle has got an active meaning /connotation.

For example-

- There is an <u>alarming</u> increase in crime.

Past participle has got a passive meaning /connotation.

For example-

- The <u>alarmed</u> soldier fled from the battlefield.

When two verb forms or action words happen to be together ,the non-finite verb will never be the main verb.

For example-

He stopped <u>laughing.</u>

I learnt <u>to drive</u>.

He liked <u>boiled</u> rice.

Types of non-finite:

1. **Infinitive**
2. **Gerund**
3. **Participle.**

All three kinds of non-finite verbs are discussed here in detail:

8.1 Infinitive

Base form of the verb (to go, to sing, to run etc.) is called infinitive.

Sometimes there is 'to' before the verb, sometimes it is 'without to'.

Ex. I want to go.   Let him go.

Types of infinitive:

1. (i)Present infinitive(to+ infinitive) to go, to do

   (ii)Negative infinitive (not+ infinitive) not to go, not to do

   He wants to go.

   They don't want to play.

2. Present continuous infinitive :(to be+…..ing) to be going, to be doing

   He seems to be following us.

3. Perfect infinitive: (to have + past participle) to have gone, to have done

   He seems to have gone from there.

 4. Perfect continuous infinitive :(to have been+….ing)to have been going, to have been doing

   They appear to have been sleeping.

   5. Present infinitive passive: to be +past participle) to be gone, to be done

   The work needs to be done.

Full infinitive and bare infinitive:

Look at these sentences-

 • **It is easy to sing.**

- **They want to go home.**

In full infinitive there are two words: to +verb

To sing, to go etc.

Now look at these sentences-

Let me tell you a story.

We saw him break the lock.

'Tell' and 'break' are also infinitive but there is no 'to' before them.

These are called bare infinitive or plain infinitive.

Uses of infinitives-

1. As subject of a verb

To advise is easy.

2. As object of a verb

We hope to start tomorrow.

3. Verb+ who/what/when/where/which/why+ infinitive.

I wonder who to invite.
Tell me when to pay.
We don't know where to stay.
Do you know how to do it?

4. Verb +object +infinitive

I told him to wait.
He requested her to sing.

5. Verb+object +to be

I consider him to be the best teacher.

He thought her to be the best singer.

6. Infinitive after certain adjectives

She was anxious to go.
I am sorry to disturb you.
I am glad to see you.

Other such adjectives are-

Angry, eager, fortunate, happy, keen, lucky, pleased, sorry, difficult, easy, glad, inclined, likely, nice, ready, surprised

7. Infinitive after certain nouns

I have no wish to change.
She has a plan to go abroad.
Other such nouns are-

Attempt, decision, demand, desire, effort, failure, promise, request

8. Infinitive of purpose

We eat to live, not live to eat.
I go there to see not to praise.

9. Infinitive after too and enough.

The box is too heavy to lift.
The shirt is too dirty to wear.
She is intelligent enough to solve the problem

Infinitive without 'to'

After modals:

I can speak English.
I will help you.

We must go now.

It might rain tonight.

After let, make, hear, and feel:

Let us go now.

I made him sing.

She heard him cry.

I felt him touch me.

Had better, would rather, sooner than etc.

You had better stop.

I would rather starve than beg.

They had sooner run than walk.

Help, know

I helped him mend his bicycle.

I have never known him lose his temper.

Practice 1 (Infinitive)

Vijaya : It will be exciting ……………(see)our old friends again.

Mrs Rao : Don't forget ………………..(keep) us informed.

Mrs rao : Are you sure you will be able……………… (Manage)?

Answer:

Vijaya: It will be exciting to see our friends again.

Mrs Rao : Don't forget to keep us informed.

Mrs Rao: Are you sure you will be able to manage?

Practice 2: Fill in the blanks using a non-finite verb-

While reading tips for health, I learnt that ………………(take) tea is not good for health .I tried ……………(think) about the ways of preventing tea . Regular intake of tea is sure …………… (injure) my health . I decided…………… (Leave) my habit of consuming tea. Once I give up tea, I am bound …………… (Improve) my health. Fully determined, I took a vow not ………… (Touch) tea again in my life.

8.2 Gerund

Gerund is a noun in the form of the present participle of a verb (that is, ending in –ing). 'Swimming' in the sentence 'I like swimming.' is a gerund. Gerund is double part of speech. It is made by adding -ing in the verb. It is made of verb and acts like a noun.

Gerunds are used in the sentence as nouns and in every way that any other noun can be used:

- Swimming is a good exercise. (subject)
- Geeta does not enjoy cooking. (direct object)
- After eating, relax for a while. (object of preposition)

Functions of a gerund in a sentence-

1. **Subject to the verb**
   - Playing badminton is my favorite pastime.
   - Smoking is injurious to health.
2. **Object to the verb**
   - I don't like smoking.
   - He preferred walking.
3. **Object to the preposition**
   - I am good at playing guitar.
   - He focused on collecting stamps.
4. **Complement to the verb**
   - My primary aim is finding a job.
   - One of the major causes of heart disease is smoking.

5. Absolute use

- Drinking being harmful, you should give it up.
- Waking early being good for health, I started it.

Gerund Phrases-

Like participles, gerunds can have a direct object.

To find out whether or not the gerund has a direct object, begin with the gerund and ask the following question:

Gerund + whom/what? = direct object

Example:

Giving the money proved a mistake.

Giving + What? = money

Money is the direct object of the gerund.

Gerund phrases can also have indirect objects:

To find out whether or not the gerund phrase has an indirect object, begin with the gerund, locate the direct object, and then ask the question **to/for whom/what?**

Example:

Giving William the money proved a mistake.

Giving + what = money (direct object)

Giving money **to/for whom? = William**

William is the indirect object of the gerund phrase.

Gerund phrases can also have prepositional phrases in them:

Giving William the money on Friday night proved a major mistake.

Since **on Friday night** tells **when?** The prepositional phrase functions as an adverb. It completes the gerund phrase.

8.3 Participle

A **participle** is a form of a verb that is used in a sentence to modify a noun, noun phrase, verb or verb phrase, and thus plays a role similar to that of an adjective or adverb.

Participles are also called verbal adjectives as they act like adjectives.

Participles are formed from a verb, ending in -ing (the present participle) or –ed,-en etc.(the past participle).

Example-

>He told me an <u>interesting</u> story. (Present Participle)
>He jumped into a <u>running</u> car. (Present Participle)
>He looked through the <u>broken</u> window. (Past Participle)
>I have to throw these <u>rotten</u> mangoes. (Past Participle)

The present participle always ends in –ing .(singing, dancing, moving, standing, walking, speaking etc.) but the past participle may have different endings .Past participle of all regular verbs end in-ed ,the past participle of irregular verbs however vary considerably. For example the past participle of verbs bring, sing, eat are brought, sung and eaten.

There are three kinds of participle-

1. Present Participle (verb +ing)

- The crying baby needed some milk.
- She does not like cooking.
- We enjoy riding on the bike every Sunday.

2. Past Participle (Third form of the verb)

- He was unable to walk with his broken leg.
- There were enough fallen leaves for the evening fire.
- The broken stem of the tree was lying on the ground.
- The newly painted building was looking very attractive .
- He traveled accompanied by his friends.
- Tired by hard work the woodcutter rested under a tree.

3. Perfect Participle (having +past participle/ having been+ third form of the verb)

- Having submitted the form the students began to study for examination.
- Having completed his work John began to walk towards coffee shop.
- Having locked the door he kept the keys in his pocket.
- Having been alone for a long time the child began to weep.
- Having been punished by the teacher the students decided to complete their assignment soon.
- Having waited for two hours she lost hope.
- Having failed twice, he did not try again.

Uses of Participles-

1. Attributive use- Participles are used before noun and qualify them.
A fallen leaf dries soon.
Your must change your torn shirt.
A lost moment never comes back.
The defeated army surrendered before the enemy.

2. Predicative use- Participle is used after the noun and qualify/modify them.
The old man seems tired.
He kept us worrying.
They marched together shouting against the leader.

3. Absolute use (When a noun or pronoun goes before a participle)-
The rain having stopped, the people came out of the homes.
The teacher being absent, the students were roaming around the canteen.
The train being late the station was full of passengers.

Practice 1
Fill in with the correct non-finite verb-forms.
(i)...............is harmful.(smoke)
(ii) My landlord is a ....fellow.(amuse)
(iii) Your performance was ....(entertain)
(iv)He loves to ....(walk)
(v) We are generally afraid of ....(die)
(vi) Your comments are ....(dishearten)
(vii) ....for the country is an honour.(fight)
(viii) Poverty presents a ....sight.(depress)
(ix) ....is the best exercise.(swim)
(x) I have a ....text of the speech.(write)
Answer-
1. Smoking   2.amusing   3. entertaining 4. Walk   5.dying
6.disheartening 7. Fighting   8.depressing   9.Swimming 10. written

9. Direct and Indirect Narration

There are two different ways in which we can report the words of a speaker.

He said, "These mangoes are sweet."
He said that those mangoes were sweet.
In the first sentence above the words of the speaker are represented in the same way as they were spoken .In the second sentence the reporter has modified the words. These two ways of expressions are named as:
    1. Direct speech or direct narration

2. Indirect speech or indirect narration

Direct speech

It contains actual words of the speaker; as

1. Sarla said, "My father has a business in Mumbai."
2. He said to me, "I am feeling unwell today."
3. She said to me, "Who teaches you English?"
4. You said to her, "Show me your frock."

In these sentences, actual words of the speaker are given within inverted commas without any change.

Indirect speech

Indirect speech gives the substance of the speaker's actual words and not the exact words spoken by him or her; as_

1. Sarla said that her father had a business in Mumbai.
2. He told me that he was feeling unwell that day.
3. She asked them who taught them English.
4. You requested her to show you her frock.

The actual words of the speaker given within inverted commas are called the Reported speech.

In the sentence 1 above '**said**' is the Reporting Verb and '**My father has a business in Mumbai**' is the Reported Speech.

Can you tell the reporting verb and reported speech in the following sentences_?

1. Radha says, "I shall finish my home work today."

2. Sushma said to Pushpa, "Show me your dolls."
3. "Have you lost your purse? " Asked my mother.
4. "I can't give you a lift", replied my neighbor.

In the direct speech

- The reported speech is put within inverted commas.
- The reported speech and the reporting verb are separated by a comma.
- The first word of the reported speech begins with a capital letter.
- In the reported speech we may use any tense required by the sense and any kind of sentence.

In the indirect speech

- Inverted commas are removed.

- The comma separating the reporting verb from the reported speech is removed.

- Reporting speech is introduced by a conjunction like that, if, what, why etc.
- Reporting verb changes according to the sense.
- The tense of the Reporting verb is never changed.
- All kind of sentences change into assertive ones.
- The mark of interrogation (?) and the mark of exclamation (!) at the end of the sentence are changed into full stop.

Rules for the change of tense

[A] If the Reporting Verb is in the Present or future Tense, the Tense of the verb in the reported speech does not change.

Examples-

1. Direct: Rajesh says, "She has bought a pen."
   Indirect: Rajesh says that she has bought a pen.

2. Direct: I say, "I spoiled all my books."
   Indirect: I say that I spoiled all my books.

3. Direct: Rajni says, "I am going to Bhopal."
   Indirect: Rajni says that she is going to Bhopal.

4. Direct: I shall say, "I went to Agra on Monday."
   Indirect: I shall say that I went to Agra on Monday.

5. Direct: He will be saying, "I remained in the lawn for an hour."
   Indirect: He will be saying that he remained in the lawn for an hour.

[B] If the reporting verb is in the past tense, the tense of the verb in the reported speech must be changed into the corresponding past tense.

Before change	After change
Present Simple	Past simple
Present continuous	past continuous
Present perfect	past perfect
present perfect continuous	past perfect continuous
past simple	past perfect
past continuous	past perfect continuous
past perfect	past perfect(No Change)
Future simple (shall/will)	should /would
Must	had to
Can	could
May	might

However the tenses may not change if the statement is **a universal truth** or is **still relevant.**

Examples-

1. I said, "I am speaking the truth."
   I said that that I was speaking the truth.
2. The teacher said, "Boys fail because they do not study regularly."
   The teacher said that boys failed because they did not study regularly.
3. We said, "They cannot cross the river."
   We said that they could not cross the river.
4. I said, "I have a good machine."
   I said that I had a good machine.
5. Raj said, "The sun rises in the east."
   Raj said that the sun rises in the east. [Exception: universal truth]

1. Present simple tense in reported speech:

When **reported speech of direct narration** has structure of **present simple tense** , it changes in **past simple tense** in **indirect narration.**

Direct Narration   : Ram said to Gopal, " I play cricket."
Indirect Narration : Ram told Gopal that he played cricket.
Direct Narration   : I said to you, "Ajay works hard."
Indirect Narration : I told you that Ajay worked hard.
Direct Narration   : We said to Meera, "The postman comes late on Saturday."
Indirect Narration : We told Meera that the postman came late on Saturday.

2. Present continuous tense in reported speech:

When **reported speech of direct narration** has structure of **present continuous tense** , it changes in **past continuous tense** in **indirect narration.**

Direct Narration   : Ajay said to Dinesh, "Your father is playing chess."

246

Indirect Narration : Ajay told Dinesh that his father was playing chess.

Direct Narration : Geeta said to Rajesh, "My friends are waiting for me."

Indirect Narration : Geeta told Rajesh that her friends were waiting for her.

Direct Narration : We said to him, "You are playing very well."

Indirect Narration : We told him that he was playing very well.

Direct Narration : They said to her, "We are inviting the mayor of the city."

Indirect Narration : They told her that they were inviting the mayor of the city.

3. Present perfect tense in reported speech:

When **reported speech of direct narration** has structure of **present perfect tense** , it changes in **past perfect tense** in **indirect narration.**

Direct Narration : You said to Rajat, "I have completed my homework."

Indirect Narration : You told Rajat that you had completed your homework.

Direct Narration : I said to him, "I have changed the content of the paper."

Indirect Narration : I told him that I had changed the content of the paper.

Direct Narration : Deepak said to me, "You have got 90 marks in Mathematics."

Indirect Narration : Deepak told me that I had got 90 marks in Mathematics.

Direct Narration : She said to her mother, "I have filled water in the bucket."

Indirect Narration : She told her mother that she had filled water in the bucket.

4. Present perfect continuous tense in reported speech:

When <u>reported speech of direct narration</u> has structure of <u>present perfect continuous tense</u> , it changes in <u>past perfect continuous tense</u> in <u>indirect narration.</u>

Direct Narration : Raj said to Deepa, " I have been working here for ten years."
Indirect Narration : Raj told Deepa that he had been working there for ten years.
Direct Narration : You said to the teacher, "I have been studying English for two hours."
Indirect Narration : You told the teacher that you had been studying English for two hours.
Direct Narration : We said to the shopkeeper, "You have been selling very good books."
Indirect Narration : We told the shopkeeper that he had been selling very good books.
Direct Narration : My father said to me, "Ajay has been bringing books for you for many weeks."
Indirect Narration : My father told me that Ajay had been bringing books for me for many weeks.

5. Past simple tense in reported speech:

When <u>reported speech of direct narration</u> has structure of <u>past simple tense</u> , it changes in <u>past perfect tense</u> in <u>indirect narration.</u>

Direct Narration : Ram said to Ajay, "I was busy yesterday."
Indirect Narration : Ram told Ajay that he had been busy the previous day.
Direct Narration : They said to my father, " Deepak got 78% in the annual examination."

Indirect Narration : They told my father that Deepak had got 78% in the annual examination.

Direct Narration : I said to Shreya, " You played very well."

Indirect Narration : I told Shreya that she had played very well.

Direct Narration : You said to your friend, "I have bought a cricket kit."

Indirect Narration : You told your friend that you had bought a cricket kit.

6. Past continuous tense in reported speech:

When **reported speech of direct narration** has structure of **past continuous tense** , it changes in **past perfect continuous tense** in **indirect narration.**

Direct Narration :Raj said, " I was waiting for my friend."

Indirect Narration : Raj said that he had been waiting for his friend.

Direct Narration : He said to Ajay, "Deepak was preparing for competitive examinations."

Indirect Narration : He told Ajay that Deepak had been preparing for competitive examinations.

Direct Narration : Sobha said to her mother, "I was washing clothes."

Indirect Narration : Sobha told her mother that she had been washing clothes .

7. Past perfect tense in reported speech:

When **reported speech of direct narration** has structure of **past perfect tense** , it remains in **past perfect tense** in **indirect narration.**

Gopal said to Ajay, "I had visited a lawyer."

Gopal told Ajay that he(Gopal) had visited a lawyer.

I said , " She had taken tea."

I said that she had taken tea.
We said, " We had not seen the Taj."
We said that we had not seen the Taj.

8. Future simple tense in reported speech:

When **reported speech of direct narration** has structure of **Future simple tense** , its helping verb 'will /shall' changes in would/should in **indirect narration.**

Direct Narration   : He said, " I will open a boutique."
Indirect Narration : He said that he would open a boutique.
Direct Narration   : She said, " I will book the tickets."
Indirect Narration : She said that she would book the tickets.
Direct Narration   : Dinesh said, " I will not travel in a train."
Indirect Narration : Dinesh said that he would not travel in a train.

9. Future continuous tense in reported speech:

When **reported speech of direct narration** has structure of **Future continuous tense** , its helping verb changes in **'should be/ would be'** in **indirect narration.**

Direct Narration   : She said , " He will be teaching in a school."
Indirect Narration : She said that he would be teaching in a school.
Direct Narration   : He said, "They will be travelling in a train."
Indirect Narration : He said that they would be travelling in a train.
Direct Narration   : Radha said, " Hari will not be playing cards."
Indirect Narration : Radha said that Hari would not be playing cards.

Rules for change of persons

[A]If the subject of reported speech is in first person it changes according to the subject of the reporting speech.

1. **Direct**:   Ram said to me, **"I** have lost the match."
   Indirect: Ram told me that **he** had lost the match.
2. **Direct**:   You said to the teacher, **"I** want some help in essay writing."
   Indirect: You told the teacher that **you** wanted some help in essay writing.

[B] If the subject of reported speech is in **second person** it changes according to the **object** of the reporting speech.

1. **Direct** :   They said to me, **"You** are our best friend."
   Indirect: They told me that **I** was their best friend.
2. **Direct**:   Ram said to Deepak, **"You** are creating problems for me."
   Indirect: Ram told Deepak that **he** (Deepak) was creating problems for him (Ram).

[C] If the subject of the reported speech is in third person it does not change.

Direct Narration: She said, **"He** is taking his examination."
Indirect Narration: She told that **he** was taking the examination.

Direct Narration: Raj said to Teena, "Your brother sings very well."
Indirect Narration: Raj told Teena that her brother sang very well.

Reported speech	Change	
subject in **first** person	Subject of reported speech changes according to **subject** of reporting speech Ram said, "I am ill." Ram told that he was ill	**S**
subject in **second**	Subject of reported speech changes according	**O**

person	to **object** of reporting speech. Ram said to me," You are my brother ." Ram told me that I was his brother.	
subject in **third** person	Subject of reported speech **does <u>not</u> change** Ram said to Mohan, "Sarla likes coffee." Ram told Mohan that Sarla liked coffee.	N

Examples: Ram said to Gopal, "You look so tired."(Direct)

Ram said to Gopal that he looked very tired. (Indirect)

I said to Juliet, "You have selected very nice dress."(Direct)

I told Juliet that she had selected very nice dress. (Indirect)

I said to John, "I will return your copy soon." (Direct)

I told John that I would return his copy soon. (Indirect)

You said to me, "Deepak is your friend."(Direct Speech)

You told me that Deepak was my friend. (Indirect Speech)

Change in some words: 'This' and 'these' are changed into 'that' and 'those' respectively. 'Shall' of the future tense changes into 'should' and 'will' of the future tense changes into 'would or should'. Words expressing nearness in time or place are generally changed into words expressing distance. For example:

Direct narration	**Indirect Narration**
Now	then
Here	there
Ago	before
Thus	so
Today	that day
Tomorrow	the next day
Yesterday	the day before
Last night	the previous night

This	that
This	that
These	those
Shall	should
Will	would or should

Change in narration in various types of sentences:

Imperative sentence A [Commands, Requests, Advises]

- Reporting verb is changed according to its sense into commanded, ordered, requested, advised, entreated, urged, forbade etc.
- Imperative mood is changed into infinitive mood by adding to before the verb.
- No conjunction is used after removing inverted commas.
- In Negative sentences 'do' is replaced by 'not to'.

Examples-

Direct: Dinesh said to me, "Please lend me your pen."
Indirect: Dinesh requested me to lend him my pen.
Direct: The teacher said to the student, "Leave the classroom."
Indirect: The teacher ordered the student to leave the classroom."
Direct: The teacher said to Mohan, "Do not return again today."
Indirect: The teacher forbade Mohan to return again that day.
Direct: Vimla said, "Be quiet and listen to the speaker."
Indirect: Vimla urged them to be quiet and listen to the speaker.
Direct: The Captain said, "March forward, soldiers."
Indirect: The captain ordered the soldiers to march forward.

Imperative sentence B [Sentences beginning with Let]

If sentence beginning with 'let' expresses suggestion then reporting verb 'said to' will change into 'proposed to' or 'suggested to' and 'let' will be replaced by 'should'.

Examples-

Direct: I said to them, "Let us go to the temple."

Indirect: I proposed to them that we should go to the temple."

Direct: Sudhir said to his wife, "Let us go to see a film."

Indirect: Sudhir suggested to his wife that they should go to see a film.

Direct : Raj said to his friends, " Let us clean the classroom."

Indirect: Raj proposed to his friends that they should clean the classroom.

Direct: The Principal said to the teachers, "Let us wait for the result."

Indirect: The Principal proposed to the teachers that they should wait for the result.

Interrogative sentence

[A] yes/no questions:

These sentences begin with auxiliary verb or modal auxiliary verb, like-

[i] Are you a student?

[ii] Will you help me?

[iii] Do you want some water?

[iv]Have you completed the story?

- To change these sentences in indirect sentence reporting verb 'said' is changed in asked or enquired.
- Conjunction 'if' or 'whether' is used before the reported speech.
- Interrogative sentence is changed into assertive sentence and interrogative mark is removed.
- Helping verb comes after subject.

Examples-

Direct – He said to Raj, "Are you going to Bhopal?"

Indirect- He asked Raj if he was going to Bhopal.

Direct- Seeta said to Meena, "Can you solve this question?"

Indirect- Seeta asked Meena if she could solve that question.

Direct- He said to me, "Has Raj given you a box?"

Indirect- He asked me whether Raj had given me a box.

Direct- My brother said to me, "Will you show me your book today?"

Indirect- My brother asked me whether I would show him my book that day.

[B] Wh-questions

• To change these sentences in indirect sentence reporting verb 'said' is changed in asked or enquired.

If first word of the reported speech is 'who', 'what', 'How', 'Where', 'Why', 'when', or 'which' then to change into indirect narration 'if' or 'whether' is not used.

• Wh- word is used as conjunction.
• Helping verb comes after subject.

Examples-

Direct – **He said to you**, "Where are you going?"

Indirect- He asked you where you were going.

Direct- I said to Raj, "Why do you play cards?"

Indirect- I asked Raj why he played cards.

Direct- They said to Geeta, "When will you reach the village?"

Indirect- They asked Geeta when she would reach the village.

Direct- You said to Meena, "Which game do you like?"

Indirect- You asked Meena which game she liked.

Exclamatory sentences

• Reporting verb is changed in exclaimed, wished, prayed, confessed, cried out, called to witness, applauded etc. according to the sense of the reporting speech.

Example-

Exclaimed with sorrow- Ah! Alas!
Exclaimed with joy- Aha! Ha ! Hurrah!
Exclaimed with surprise- Oh! What! How!
  Exclaimed with contempt- Pooh! Pshaw!
  Exclaimed with regret- Sorry!
  Applauded saying… - Bravo! Hear!

- What and how is replaced with very or great.
- Inverted commas are removed and that is added.
- Words such as' Hurrah', 'Wow', and 'Alas' are removed.
- Exclamatory sentence is changed into Assertive sentence.

Direct: The captain said, "Hurrah! We have won!"
Indirect: The captain exclaimed with joy that they had won the match.
Direct: He said, "How beautiful this painting is!"
Indirect: He exclaimed with delight that that painting was very beautiful.

Optative sentences (Expessing wish)

- Reporting verb is changed in wished or prayed.
- Commas before reporting speeches are removed and conjunction 'that' is used.
- Optative sentence is changed into assertive sentence.

Examples-

  Direct – He said to me, "May you live long!"
  Indirect- He wished that I might live long.

Direct- He said, "If I were a king!"
Indirect- He wished that he would be a king.
Direct- She said, "If I had a fifty rupee note!"
Indirect- She wished that she would have a fifty rupee note.

Direct- Radha said to me, "Would that you were here at that time!"
Indirect-Radha wished that I had been there at that time

Narration: Various Examples

Direct Narration	Indirect Narration
1 Ram said to me, "I have lost the match."	1. Ram told me that he had lost the match.
2 They said to me, "You are our best friend."	2. They told me that I was their best friend.
3 Ram said to him, "You are creating problems for me."	3. Ram told me that I was creating problem for him.
4 You said to the teacher, "I want some help in essay writing."	4. You told the teacher that you wanted some help in essay writing.
5 We said to the principal, "Some students want morning classes in school.	5. We told the principal that some students wanted morning classes in school.

Examples:

Direct Narration	Indirect Narration
1. I said to him, "Your sister is absent in school for many days."	1. I told him that his sister was absent in school for many days.
2. They said to me, "We have arrived in the town."	2. They told me that they had arrived in the town.
3. He said, "I am going to the pictures."	3. He told that he was going to the pictures.
	4. Rana says that Sita will dance.

4. Rana says, "Sita will dance." 5. Mohan will say, "I want two persons to help me."	5. Mohan will say that he wants two persons to help him.

Examples:

	Direct Narration	Indirect Narration
1	She said, "He is taking his examination."	1. She told that he was taking examination.
2	The teacher said to me, "What are you doing?"	2. The teacher asked me what I was doing.
3	He said to me," Do you know the way."	3. He asked me if I knew the way.
4	Mahan asked, "Are the boys here?	4. Mohan asked if the boys were there.
5	He asked me, "Can you see me tomorrow?"	5. He asked me if I could see him the next day.
6	He said, "Is Raju your brother?"	6. He asked if Raju was my brother.
7	They said to the principal, "Are we going to take part in the essay competition?"	7. They asked the principal if they were going to take part in the essay competition.

Examples:

Direct Narration	Indirect Narration

1	You asked, "Where is my pen?"	1. You asked where your pen was.
2	She said, "Do you know who is coming?"	2. She asked if I knew who was coming.
3	The teacher asked the student, "How did you solve this problem?"	3. The teacher asked the student how he had solved that problem.
4	He said, "Alas, I am ruined."	4. He exclaimed with sorrow that he was ruined.
5	She said, "What a fine picture it is!"	5. She exclaimed with joy that it was a very fine picture.

Examples:

Direct Narration	Indirect Narration
1 Sita said, "How clever I am!"	1. Sita exclaimed with pride that she was very clever.
2 He said to me, "May God bless you!"	2. He wished for me that God might bless me.
3 He said, "What a fool Seema is!	3. He exclaimed that Seema was a big fool.
4 A guest said, "What a nice man Mr.Prasad is!	4. A guest remarked with appreciation that Mr Prasad was a very nice person.
5 "What a lot of food there is to eat!" She said.	5. She exclaimed with joy that there was a lot of food to eat.
6 They said, "Hurrah! We have won the match!	6. They exclaimed with delight that they had won the match.

Exercise:

Change into indirect Narration:

1. He said to me, "My home is in Delhi.
2. They said to me, "You have answered a question."

3. Raju said to Gopal, "I need your copy."
4. They said to you, "Rajesh is going to market.
5. I said to you, "Ram lives in Mumbai."
6. I said to him, "I have five rupees."
7. I said to her," Do you know English?"
8. I said to them, "Have you taken tea?"
9. You said to him, "Are you writing a letter?"
10. You said to them, "Is your brother coming here?"
11. You said to her, "Am I looking good?"
12. You said to me, "Where do you live?"
13. We said to her, "What is your name?"
14. We said to you, "When do you get up?"
15. We said to him, "Which pen do you like?"
16. We said to them, "Why do you go to market?"
17. Ram said to Laxman, "Kill that demon."
18. I said to Mohan. "Open the door."
19. We said to Geeta, "Take you T.C. and go home."
20. You said to me, "Write all the answer."
21. Ravi said to Meera, "Don't show you copy."
22. She said to me, "Don't go anywhere."
23. Hari said to DInesh , "Please bring my bag."
24. I said to Seema, " please take this book."
25. Gopal said to the king, " I can bring a hilsa."
26. The king said to him, " Go and bring a hilsa."
27.The man said to the king , "I was your enemy".
28.The boy said to Kari, "Did you steal bananas?"
29. Hari said to his father," Please give me ten rupees."
30. We asked Raj, "What is your pet's name?
31. She said to Mamta, "May you pass the exam!"
32. The King said, "What a beautiful scene this is!"
33. He said, "Let us play cricket."
34. The teacher said, "Open the door."
35. The minister said to the king, "Please begin the ceremony."

Answers-

1. He told me that his home was in Delhi.
2. They told me the I had answered a question.
3. Raju told Gopal that he needed his(Gopal's) copy.
4. They told me that Ramesh was going to market.
5. I told you that Ram lived in Mumbai.
6. I told him that I had five rupees.
7. I asked her if she knew English.
8. I asked them if they had taken tea.
9. You asked them were they writing a letter.
10. You asked them if their brother was coming there.
11. You asked her if you were looking good.
12. You asked me where I lived.
13. We asked her what her name was.
14. We asked him when he got up.
15. We asked him which pen he liked.
16. We asked them why they went to market.
17. Ram ordered Laxman to kill that demon.
18. I ordered Mohan to open the door.
19. We suggested Geeta to take her T.C.and go home.
20. You asked me to write all the answers.
21. Ravi forbade Meera to go anywhere.
22 . She forbade me to go anywhere.
23. Hari requested Dinesh to bring his copy.
24. I requested Seema to take that book.
25. Gopal told the king that he could bring Hilsa fish.
26. The king ordered him to go and bring a Hilsa fish..
27. The man told the king that he (the man) was his enemy.
28. The boy asked Kari if he stole the bananas.
29. Hari requested his father to give him ten rupees.
30. We asked Raj what his pet's name was.
31. She wished that Mamta might pass the exam.
32. The king exclaimed with delight that it was a beautiful scene.
33. He suggested to us to play cricket.
34. The teacher ordered to open the door.
35. The minister requested the king to begin the ceremony.

10. Three Types of Sentences

According to their grammatical structure sentences can be classified into three types-

1. Simple sentence.   2. Compound sentence   3.Complex sentence

1. Simple sentence-

A simple sentence has only one clause, i.e. one subject and one predicate, e.g.

The students are learning grammar.
I am taking tea.
The Train starts at 6.30 p.m.
He had sold all bags.

2. Compound sentence

The compound sentence is made up of one Principal Clause and at least one Coordinate Clause. The Coordinate clause must be of equal status with Principal clause.

Coordinate conjunctions used to combine coordinate clause with principal clause are- And, but, or, nor, either-or, neither-or, for, still, otherwise, else, either, both-and, not only-but also.

Example-

The child ran fast **and** won the race.
He is slow, **but** he is sure.
Work hard , **or** you will fail.
He didn't come **nor** did he send any message.
Either be attentive, **or** leave the class.
Neither Raj came **nor** did he send any message.
He **neither** drinks **nor** smokes.
He is **not only** careless **but also** obstinate.
I listened eagerly, **for** he sang my favorite song.
He is rude, **still** he had many friends.
He remained sick during the test, **still** he got the highest marks.
Work hard, **otherwise** you will fail.
Hari works hard and **therefore** stands first.
Walk quickly, **else** you will not catch the train.
Submit the assignment in time, **else** the teacher will not accept it.
Both my mother **and** my father were present there.

3. Complex sentence-Complex sentence is made of one principal clause and at least one subordinate clause. The subordinate clause is of three types-

a) Noun Clause.
b) Adjective Clause
c) Adverb Clause

Examples-

The boy who is sitting under the tree is my brother.
I do not know whether he has passed or not.

I do not know where Ramesh lives.
Listen to what I say.

Practice 1

Identify these sentences by choosing (a) Simple, (b) Compound or (c) Complex.

1. The hostels of these students look crowded.

a. Simple
b. compound
c. complex
2. Their sports ground is full of dust and their players are rarely well equipped.

a. Simple
b. compound
c. complex
3. They use simple bats made locally rather than branded ones.

a. Simple
b. compound
c. complex
4. Although the schools of big cities have better facilities, they rarely produce any national level player.

a. Simple
b. compound
c. complex
5. The government provides facilities for rural schools but they rarely reach the deserving hands.

a. Simple
b. compound
c. complex

Answer

Practice 1

1.a   2.b   3.a   4.c   5.b

11. Complex Sentences

Complex sentence has one main clause and one or more subordinate clause, e.g.

i) I read the book which I had bought from the Book Fair.

ii)The person who is standing there is my uncle.

In the above sentence (i) 'I read the book' is main clause while the clause 'which I bought from the fair' is subordinate clause. These clauses together make a complex sentence.

Subordinate clauses are of three kinds:

A] Noun Clause
B] Adjective clause (Relative clause)
C] Adverb clause

These clauses are discussed here in detail:

Noun Clause

Noun clause functions as nouns in relation to the main clause. These clauses function as

1. Subject of the verb.

    a. That the Earth is round is a fact.
    b. His words makes me angry.
    c. That he is ill is not true.
    d. Where he lives is not known to me.
    e. What he said is wrong.
    f. Whom God loves die young.
    g. Why he has not come is a mystery.
    h. How she could marry her son was her chief concern.
    i. When he will come back is known to his father.
    j. What you did was against the law.
    k. Who helps himself is helped by God.
    l. Anything he says makes her uneasy.

In the first sentence the noun clause (underlined part) is the subject of the verb 'is' in the main clause.

2. Object of the transitive verb

    a. I firmly **believe** that he will tell me the truth.
    b. I **know** where he lives.
    c. **Tell** me where the post office is.
    d. I do not **know** when father will return.
    e. I **think** you are right.
    f. The teacher **demonstrated** how the practical was to be done.
    g. She **hopes** she will get first division.
    h. She **fears** that she would fail in the examination.

In the above sentences the noun clause (underlined part) is the object of the verb (in bold letters) of the main clause.

3. Complement of the verb.

a. It seems <u>that the students are tired</u>.
b. This is <u>where I live.</u>
c. Her problem is <u>how she can become a doctor</u>.
d. My belief is <u>that she will not come</u>.
e. It seems <u>that the guests are very pleased</u>.
f. This is <u>what I expected</u>.
g. I have <u>what I want</u>.

In the first sentence the noun clause (underlined part) is the complement of the verb 'seems' in the main clause.

4. Case in apposition

a. It is a fact <u>that the earth goes round the sun</u>.
b. One must always remember this, <u>that honesty is the best policy.</u>
c. It is feared <u>that she would not come</u>.
d. It was unfortunate <u>that you were present at the scene of crime.</u>
e. Her great fear is <u>that she would fail</u>.
f. My wish is <u>that you may get success soon.</u>

In the first sentence the noun clause is in apposition with the noun 'fact' in the main clause.

5. Object of the preposition

a. We must pay attention to <u>what our elders tell us.</u>
b. I do not believe in <u>what he says</u>.
c. He was punished for <u>what he had done.</u>
d. Your career depends on <u>how you work.</u>
e. Trust on <u>what your father tells you.</u>
f. Will the chair sell for <u>what it is worth?</u>
g. She was greatly annoyed by <u>what I told her.</u>
h. Why was he not grateful for <u>the help I provided him?</u>

In the first sentence the noun clause is the object of the preposition 'to' in the main clause.

Adjective Clause

Adjective clause (relative clause)-Adjective clause describes a noun or a pronoun in the main clause or in other subordinate clause. These clauses are introduced by relative pronouns like who, whom, which, whose, that e.g.,

i) The house **which has large glass windows** was burgled yesterday.
The adjective clause describes the noun 'house' in the main clause.
ii) I know the boy **who won the national championship.**
The adjective clause describes the noun 'boy' in the main clause.
iii) He **who laughs last** laughs best.
The adjective clause describes the pronoun 'He' in the main clause.

(iv)This is the picture that was drawn by him.
(v) The time when he comes here is not known.
(vi) The boy who is sitting next to me is Raj.
(vi) I met a man who was a poet.
(vii) The park which is located at the back of my house has lovely flowers.
(viii)I saw the place where the truck had an accident.

Adverb Clause

Adverb clause –Adverb clause functions as an adverb in relation to the main clause or other clauses. They may modify the verb or an adjective or another adverb by telling about their time, place, condition, purpose, result, and manner etc., e.g.

1. Adverb Clause of Time

a) I met him **when** he was going home.

b) The lawyer always comes **whenever** he is sent for.

c) **When** you have submitted your assignment you may go home.

(d) He will join us **when** he is free.

(e)Make hay **while** the sun shines.

(f) **As** she entered the room, all stood up to greet her.

(g)She left **after** she had finished her work.

(h)Think **before** you speak.

(i)He has been happy **since** he joined the office.

(j)The train must wait **till** the signal is red.

(k)**So long as** I am here you need not worry.

(l)**As soon as** the bell rung the students came out of the classes.

(m)Do not start the game **till** the signal is given.

(n) It is dull in our house **since** my parents departed.

(o)**Just** as the bell rang the teacher entered the class.

(p)**No sooner** did he leave the room **than** the rain started.

In the above sentences temporal adverbial clause usually begin with: when, whenever, while, as, after, since, before, till, as soon as, no sooner...than, so long as etc. These conjunctions combine the main clause with the adverb clause of time.

2. Adverb Clause of Place

a) You will find your book **where** you kept it.

(b) We do not know **where** to apply.

(c)You should follow him **wherev**er he goes.

(d)I shall reach **wherever** you want me to come.

(e) She does not know **whither** she should go.

(f) You should search your ring **where** you last stayed.

(g) I have forgotten **where** I kept my copy.

(h)**Wherever** he goes his misfortune follows him.

In the above sentences adverb clause of place begin with conjunctions 'where', 'wherever', 'whither' etc.

3. Adverb Clause of Reason

(a) The students are happy **because** they have passed the examination.

(b) She failed **because** she did not work hard.

(c)**Since** you say so, I must believe it.

(d)**As** he was not there, I spoke to his brother.

(e)I am glad **that** you have come.

(f) He is absent **as** he is sick today.

(g) I am very pleased **that** you qualified the test.

(h)**As** he was absent, he couldn't receive the reward.

(i) **Since** your father is not at home, you may receive the letter.

(j) **Because** they are rich, they live luxurious life.

(k) I am relieved **that** you reached in time.

(l) **Since** you are the captain you may receive the trophy.

In the above sentences adverb clause of reason begin with because, since, that, as, etc.

4. Adverb clause of condition

a) **If** you work hard you will surely succeed.

(b) **If** I make a promise, I keep it.

(c) **Unless** you work hard, you will fail.

(d) You will need an umbrella **in case** it rains.

(e) **Whether** we win **or** lose we must do our best.

(f) I can go **provided** you pay my fare.

(g) We will get the reservation **provided** he reaches in time.

(h) We cannot qualify **unless** we work hard.

(i) We shall go to see the movie **if** the weather is fine.

(j) He will forgive **on condition** that you promise not to repeat the mistake.

In the above sentences adverb clause of condition begin with if, unless, whether...or, in case, provided, on condition, etc.

5. Adverb Clause of Purpose

(a) You must work hard **so that** you may score high marks.
(b) We eat **that** we may live.
(c) Note it down **lest** you forget it.
(d) Take the route chart with you **so that** you may find the way easily.
(e) Identity card is issued **so that** the unauthorized persons may not enter.
(f) Walk carefully **lest** you should fall down.
(g) Move quickly **lest** we should miss the plane.
(h) Work hard **so that** you may pass.

Adverb clause of purpose are generally introduced by that, in order that, so that, lest, in case etc.

6. Adverb Clause of Result

(a) He worked **so** hard **that** he stood first in class.
(b) **So** great a storm arose **that** all the ships were wrecked.
(c) He spoke in **such** a way **that** no one understood him.
(d) It is **so** common **that** even a child knows it.
(e) He is **such** a gentleman **that** all believe him.
(f)The fire was **so** great **that** all the shops were burnt.
(g)It rained **so** heavily **that** the river was soon above the mark.
(h) He danced in **such** a way **that** the audience was mesmerized.
(i) The earthquake was **so** powerful **that** thousands of buildings collapsed.

In the above sentences 'that' preceded by 'so' or 'such' in the modified clause introduces the adverb clause.

7. Adverb clause of supposition/concession

a) **Though** he is very clever, he is not very popular.
(b)**Even if** it rains, we must start.

(c) **Though** he is poor he is honest.

(d)**Though** she is rich she is a miser.

(e)He left the room **though** it was raining then.

(f) **Although** they were tired they worked all night.

(g)**Even if** he is aged he is regular in his morning walk.

(h)**Although** I have refused him he entered again.

Some more examples:

- **Whether** he comes **or** not we shall start the game at 5 p.m.
- **Whatever** they may say I shall do I consider right.
- **However** late the train comes I will reach before evening.
- **Though** she is poor, she is always neatly dressed.
- **Though** you hate me, I shall help you.
- I will play **even if** you forbid me do.
- **Even if** I fail I will try again and again until I get success.
- **While** I admire your courage, I think you should avoid such a dangerous journey.
- **Where** Raj has many critics his brother is very popular.

In the above sentences the adverb clause is introduced by conjunctions 'though', 'although', 'even if' 'however', 'whether....or not', 'no matter', 'not withstanding' etc.

8. Adverb Clause of Degree/comparison

When 'manner' is the point of comparison the clause is introduced by 'as'

a) It happened as I told you.

b) Do to others as you wish them to do to you.

When 'degree' is the point of comparison, another 'as' or 'so' is used in the preceding clause.

c) She is as wise as she is beautiful.

d) He is not so rich as he appears

e) He is not **as** tall **as** you (are).

Use of 'the' with comparatives in both clauses:

(f) The sooner you come, the better it will be for you.

(g)The more he gets, the more he wants.

Use of 'than' in modifying clause:

(h)She is older than she looks.

(i)I could do no better than I did.

Sometimes a verb in the adverb clause is omitted or understood:

(j)He is much better than you (are).

(k) No one teaches better than Mr. Sharma(does).

9. Adverb Clause of Manner

a) You must do **as** you are told. [Adverb clause of manner]

b) This is **how** he did it.

c) She is a good painter **as** we know her.

d) He did **as** we told him.

e) **As** you sow, so you reap.

The words 'as', 'how' etc. are sub –ordinate conjunctions denoting manner. They introduce the adverb clause of manner.

10. Adverb Clause of Contrast

a) She cannot climb that hill **however** hard shy may try.

b) He is honest **though** he is poor.

c) **Though** he worked hard, he failed.

d) **Though** he is rich, he is humble.

e) **However** fast you drive, you can't reach before evening.

f) **Even though** the weather was hot he didn't use a.c.

g) **Though** he was tired he completed his work.

h) **While** Anil is frank his twin brother Nilesh is shy.

i) **Whereas** Shimla is cold Jaipur is a hot place.

j) The girls had not revised the course properly **yet** they got good marks.

The words 'however', 'though' "even though' 'Whereas' etc. are subordinate conjunctions denoting contrast. These conjunctions introduce the adverb clause of contrast.

Practice 1. Join these separate sentences into <u>complex sentences</u> using the words in brackets-

1. Don't eat too much. You will be ill. (If)
2. You are strong. I am equally strong. (as.........as)
3. He began late. He finished fast. (though)
4. Nobody likes him. He is very dishonest. (because)
5. The bell rang. They all came up at once.(as soon as)
6. I will get ready. Wait till then. (Till)
7. He is poor. He is honest in spite of it. (Though)
8. I met my old friend .He is now an officer. (Who)
9. I must know all the facts. I cannot help you otherwise. (before)
10. This is the boy .His parents are teachers. (Whose)
11. You must work hard. Otherwise you won't pass. (Unless)

Answers (Practice 1)

1. If you eat too much you will be ill.
2. You are as strong as I am.
3. Though he began late he finished fast.
4. Nobody likes him because he is very dishonest.
5. As soon as the bell rang they all came out.
6. Wait till I get ready.
7. Though he is poor he is honest.
8. I met my old friend who is now an officer.
9. Before I can help you I must know all the facts.
10. This is the boy whose parents are teachers.
11. Unless you work hard you won't pass.

Practice 2.Fill in the blanks choosing correct conjunction from the bracket.

1. Nothing happened ………we have feared.(since, as, though)
2. He is the man……….we all respect.(which, whom, how)
3. Do it………….you forget it.(before, after, that)
4. We love them ………..love us.(where, who, whom)
5. He is older …………..he looks.(as, than ,as if)
6. You may come………….you like.(as if ,if ,until)
7. I did it…………I had to do it.(though ,unless, because)
8. I read the book………..I was in hospital.(because, if, while)

Answers (Practice 2)

1. Nothing happened as we have feared.
2. He is the man whom we all respect.
3. Do it before you forget it.
4. We love them who love us.
5. He is older than he looks.
6. You may come if you like.
7. I did it because I had to do it.
8. I read the book while I was in hospital.

Practice3

Combine these sentences-
1. He entered the room.
   I was taking tea.(when)
2. We will leave.
   The taxi arrives.(as soon as)
3. The dog barks.
   He hears the bell.(whenever)

Answer-
1. He entered the room when I was taking tea.
2. As soon as taxi arrives we will leave.
3. The dog barks whenever he hears the bell.

Practice 4: Combine these pairs of sentences using the subordinate conjunctions given against them:

(i) The telephone bell rang.

    I was going to bed at that time.   (when)

(ii) Don't talk.

    She is singing. (while)

(iii) Do it.

    You forget it.(before)

(iv) They will play cricket.

    We will play football.(while)

(v) I will send you the ticket.

    I will get it.(as soon as)

(vi) The public became silent.

    The leader rose to speak.(as)

(vii) I haven't met him.

    I came to live here.(since)

(viii) The beggar won't go away.

    You will give him some money.(until)

(ix) We reached the station.

    The train had left.(after)

(x)   There is unity in our country.

    We will remain strong.(as long as)

Answer-

    (i) The telephone bell rang when I was going to bed.

    (ii) Don't talk while she is singing.

    (iii) Do it before you forget it.

    (iv) They will play cricket while we will play football.

    (v) I will send you the ticket as soon as I will get it.

    (vi) The public became silent as the leader rose to speak.

    (vii) I haven't met him since I came to live here.

    (viii) The beggar won't go away until you will give him some money.

    (ix)We reached the station after the train had left.

    (x)As long as there is unity in our country we will remain strong.

Practice5. Make complex sentence from these pairs of simple sentences:

(i) He won't pay it.
   You send him the bill again. (unless)
(ii) You work harder.
   You will fail.   (unless)
(iii) Work well.
    You want quick payment. (if)
(iv) I will go.
    You accompany me.   (if)
(v) The boy is Rohit.
   The boy is sitting next to me. (who)
(vi) The girl is his sister.
    You met the girl at the door. (Whom)
(vii) He takes bath.
    The sun rises.(as soon as)
(viii) We will not eat food.
    She does not serve food.(unless)
(ix) I like it.
    I shall buy it. (if)

Answers:
(i) He won't pay unless you send him the bill again.
(ii) Unless you work harder you will fail.
(iii)Work well if you want quick payment.
(iv) I will go if you accompany me.
(v) The boy who is sitting next to me is Rohit.
(vi)The girl whom you met at the door is his sister.
(vii) He takes bath as soon as the sun rises.
(viii) We will not eat food unless she serves it.
(ix) If I like it I shall buy it.

Practice 6.Combine the following sentences using the subordinators of contrast clause-

1. Smokers fight for the right to smoke in public places.

Non smokers fight for the right to clean air.
2. The environment is polluted in urban areas.
   The environment is clean in many rural areas.
3. Scientists know the reasons of earthquakes.
   They are still not able to predict them.
4. Population growth is a real problem.
   The government has been slow to take action to check it.

Practice7. Combine the given pairs of sentences:

1.He said something. You didn't hear it.
2.A writer wrote this story. He is coming our home this evening.
3. The boy is crying. His watch has been lost.
4.This is house. We live in it.
5. The girl is my student. She came here in the morning.
6.How will he finish the work in time? I don't know.
7.What is your opinion ?Please let me know.
8. Rahul bought a watch. It has a gold dial.
9. My uncle works somewhere. I don't know the place.
10.He will win the race. It is sure.

Answers:

1. You didn't hear what he said.
2. The writer who wrote this story is coming our home this evening.
3. The boy whose watch has been lost is crying.
4. This is the house where we live.
5. The girl who came here in the morning is my student.
6. I don't know how he will finish the work in time
7. Please let me know what your opinion is.
8. Rahul bought a watch which has a gold dial.
9. I don't know where my uncle works.
10. It is sure that he will win the race.

11.1 Conditional Sentences

(If-Clauses Type I and II)

Conditional sentences are complex sentences which consist of two clauses. One is main clause and the other is subordinate clause. The subordinate clause here is conditional sentence. The condition of the subordinate clause affects the main clause.

Conditional Sentences are also known as Conditional Clauses or If Clauses. They are used to express that the action in the main clause (without *if*) can only take place if a certain condition (in the clause with *if*) is fulfilled. There are two types of Conditional Sentences.

Conditional Sentence Type 1
These sentences give the sense that it is possible and also *very likely* that the condition will be fulfilled.

Form-

If+ simple present, Future simple (Will+ infinitive)

Example: If you call him, he will come immediately.

The main clause can also be at the beginning of the sentence. In this case, don't use a comma.

Example: He will come immediately if you call him.

Sometimes the 'main clause' and 'if clause' are negative.

If you don't complete your work, you may not get a chocolate.

Use-

Conditional Sentences Type I refer to the future. An action in the future will only happen if a certain condition is fulfilled by that time. We don't know for sure whether the condition actually will be fulfilled or not, but the conditions seems rather realistic – so we think it is likely to happen.

Example:

- If you come in time, we shall go to watch a movie.

  Here time is the decisive factor. The simple condition is friend's arrival in time .Since it is very much possible so the situation is realistic here.

More examples:

1. We will have fun if we go to the cinema.
2. If you get good marks you will get admission in a good college.
3. If I have the time, I shall study more.
4. If she feels ill, she will not go to work.
5. If it rains, we shall cancel our trip.

Sometimes the connective (if/whether) is omitted; this happens when the modifying clause precedes the modified clause and/or there is inversion in the modifying clause:

Had you come earlier, you would have met him.
(You would have met him, if you had come earlier.)
They would be happier, were they more sincere.

(If they were more sincere)

Practice 1. Combine these sentences using 'if'.

(i)You will win the prize. You play well.

(ii)I shall pay you more money. You work well.

(iii) It rains. They can't play.

(iv) India may win this match. They players play with team spirit.

(v)You will not pass .You do not study.

(vi)The principal will accept his application. He applies in time.

(vii) Water changes into vapor. It is boiled.

(viii) You will get the train. You reach in time.

Answers-

(i) If you play well you will win the prize.

(ii) If you work well I shall pay you more money.

(iii) If it rains they can't play.

(iv) India may win the match if the players play with team spirit.

(v)If you do not study you will not pass.

(vi)The principal will accept his application if he applies in time.

(vii) Water changes into vapor if it is boiled.

(viii) You will get the train if you reach in time.

Conditional Sentence Type 2

These sentences give the sense that

"It is possible but very unlikely, that condition will be fulfilled."

Form-

If+ simple past, conditional (would +infinitive)

Example: If I reached in time, I would see her.

The main clause can also be at the beginning of the sentence. In this case, don't use a comma.

Example: I would see her if I reached in time.

 Sometimes the 'Main clause' and / or 'if clause' might be negative.

Example: If I did not study, I would fail the exam.

Were instead of Was

In 'If Clauses Type II', we usually use 'were'– even if the pronoun is *I, he, she* or *it* –.

Example: If I **were** you, I would not do this.

Use

Conditional Sentences Type II refers to situations in the present. An action could happen if the present situation were different. I don't really expect the situation to change, however. I just imagine *„ what would happen if ... "*

Example:

I would see her if I reached in time

I would like to see a friend. I have tried to reach in time, but I could not reach there in time. So now I think it is rather unlikely that I will eventually see her.

Example:

- If I had money, I would go to Kashmir on my holidays.
- They would look for a job if they had already finished school.
- If he were interested in having a part-time job, I would get him one.
- You would feel better if you did not eat so much.
- He would earn a lot of money if he worked harder.
- The flowers would not have faded if the gardener had watered them.
- If you had run you would have caught the bus.

12. Compound Sentences

- When two clauses are independent of each other and are of equal rank .Such clauses are called co-ordinate clauses.
- A sentence made up of co-ordinate clauses is a compound sentence.
- The clauses forming a compound sentence are joined by a coordinating conjunction.

Coordinating conjunctions-

1. Cumulative conjunctions
2. Adversative conjunctions
3. Alternative conjunctions
4. Illative conjunctions

1. Cumulative conjunctions-

These **conjunctions** add one statement or a fact with another. The main cumulative conjunctions are-

and, both…and, too, not only…but also, as well as

Examples-

1. She is **both** beautiful and intelligent.
2. He is **not only** rich **but also** clever.
3. Mohan is reading **and** his sister is cooking.
4. He **as well as** his parents is illiterate.
5. Hercules was tall and strong **too.**
6. The robbers **not only** took away all the cash from the ATM **but also** set fire to it.

2. Adversative conjunctions –

These conjunctions show opposition or contrast between two statements.

Ex- but, still, yet, nevertheless, only, whereas, while, etc.

Examples-

1. Do what you like, **only** do not sit near me.
2. My uncle is rich, **whereas** my father is poor.
3. I felt angry, **but** I kept quiet.
4. He worked hard, **yet** he failed.
5. He worked hard, **nevertheless** he failed.
6. He is poor **still** he is happy.

3. Alternative conjunctions

Alternative conjunction expresses a choice between two alternatives. Such conjunctions are-

or, either …or, neither …nor, otherwise, nor, neither, else.

Examples-

1. **Either** you **or** Mohan is at fault.
2. He has **neither** a scooter **nor** a car.
3. Hurry **or** (else) you will miss the train.
4. Work hard, **otherwise** you will fail
5. She didn't come; **neither** did she send any message.
6. You must **either** keep quiet **or** leave the class.
7. You can have tea **or** fruit juice.

4. Illative conjunctions

Conjunctions which express an inference are called illative conjunctions.

Illative conjunctions show that one statement or fact is inferred, or proved from another. They, therefore, express inference. They are-

Therefore, so   , for   , then

Examples-

1. He worked hard **so** he passed.
2. The bus is about to go let us get in **then.**
3. The days are short **for** it is December.
4. We read the letter eagerly **for** it brought news of our lost motorbike.
5. She is only 16 **therefore** not eligible for votes.

Examples of compound sentences:

The two simple sentences are given below. They can be combined into a compound sentence as they both are of equal rank.

- The sun rose.
- The fog disappeared.

The sun rose **and** the fog disappeared.

Let us see another example-

- He struck me.
- I fell down.

He struck me **and** I fell down.

Some more examples-

- I called on you yesterday.
- You were not at home.

I called on you yesterday **but** you were not at home.

- He is rich.
- He leads an unhappy life.

He is rich **but** he leads an unhappy life.

- He is intelligent
- He is hard working.

He is **both** intelligent **and** hardworking.

- He is a poet.
- He is a singer.

He is **both** a poet **and** a singer.

- He was punished.
- He was fined.

He was **not only** punished **but also** fined.

- Mark is a good bowler.
- He is a good batsman.

Mark is **not only** a good bowler **but also** a good batsman.

- He went to see a picture.
- His father also went to see a picture.

He **as well as** his father went to see a picture.

- My marriage will take place in April.
- If it does not, it will take place in October.

My marriage will take place **either** in April **or** in October.

- I will not go to Srinagar.
- I will not go to Bangalore.

I will go **neither** to Srinagar **nor** to Bangalore.

- I do not like coffee.
- I do not like tea.

I like **neither** tea **nor** coffee.

- He is poor.
- He is contented with his lot.

He is poor **yet** he is contented with his lot.

- I like this book.
- I bought it.

I like this book **therefore** I bought it.

- I cannot help her.
- I have no money.

I have no money **therefore** I cannot help her.

- She kept waiting till late at night.
- He did not come back.

She kept on waiting till late at night, **however**, he did not come back.

- Run fast.
- You will miss the train.

Run fast **or** you will miss the train.

- Walk carefully.
- You may fall.

Walk carefully **otherwise** you may fall.

Practice 1

Join the following sentences into <u>compound sentences</u> using the words in brackets:

1. She must weep .She will die. (or)
2. He is slow. He is sure. (but)
3. Rajeev worked hard. He won a scholarship. (and)
4. I went to his house. I did not meet him. (but)
5. He is very rich. He is unhappy. (yet)
6. You should learn how to read English. You should learn how to speak English. (not only......but also)
7. He was punished. He was fined also. (as well as).
8. Do not do this. Do not do that. (neither.........nor)
9. He cried .He wept. (both...........and)
10. Correct your habits .You will suffer. (else/otherwise)

 Answers (Practice 1)

1. She must weep, or she will die.
2. He is slow, but he is sure.
3. Rajeev worked hard and won a scholarship.

4. I went to his house but did not meet him.

5. He is very rich, yet he is unhappy.

6. You should learn not only how to read English but also how to speak English.

7. He was punished as well as fined.

8. Neither do this nor that.

9. He both cried and wept.

10. Correct your habits otherwise you will suffer.

Practice 2

Fill in the blank with right words from brackets-

1. Work hard ………..you will fail. (unless ,or, and)

2. He is poor ……… he is honest.(while, yet, as well as)

3. He neither drinks…………..smokes.(or, nor, end)

4. Many of us can read English…….can't speak it. (and ,or, but)

5. He worked ………..hard………..he fell ill. (as………if, so……..that, as……..that)

Answers (Practice 2)

1. Work hard or you will fail.

2. He is poor, yet he is honest.

3. He neither drinks nor smokes.

4. Many of us can read English but can't speak it.

5. He worked so hard that he fell ill.

Practice 3

Rewrite using 'no sooner……than'.

1. As soon as he died, his sons quarreled over his property.

2. They had come and we started for the film.

3. As soon as she heard her result she fainted.

4. I reached the school. The bell rang.

5. As soon as she looks at me, she smiles.

Answer-

1. No sooner did he die than his sons quarreled over his property.
2. No sooner had he come than we started for the film.
3.No sooner did she hear her result than she fainted.
4.No sooner did I reach the school then the bell rang.
5.No sooner does she look at me than she smiles.

Practice 4:
Do as directed-

1.Combine using 'neither………..nor'
  a. We do not lend anything.
  b. We do not borrow anything.
2.Combine using ' neither ………nor'-
  He did not ring me.
  He did not write me.
  3. Combine using 'no sooner…………than .
    a.The teacher entered the room.
    b.The boys became quiet.
  4. Combine into complex sentence using ' as soon as.'
    I saw the tiger.
    I ran away.
  5. Combine using 'no sooner…. than'.
    a. He reached the station.
    b. The train arrived.
  6. Combine using 'as soon as'.
    a. The train arrived.
    b. The passengers began to move.

Answers-
1. We neither lend not borrow anything.
2. She neither rang not wrote to me.
3. No sooner did the teacher enter the room than the boys became quiet.
4. As soon as I saw the tiger I ran away.
5. No sooner did he reach the station than the train arrived.
6. As soon as the train arrived the passengers began to move.

Practice 5:

Join the following separate sentences into compound sentences using the words in brackets:

1. She is slow. She is sure.(but)
2. Raju failed twice. He would not stop. (yet)
3. Seema worked hard.She secured first position.(and)
4. She cried.She wept.(both….and)
5.They were punished.They were fined.(both…and)
6.Do not play carom.Do not play ludo.(neither…not)
7.Mend your ways. You will suffer.(or)
8.He gave him shelter.He shared his secrets with him.(not only…but also)
9.He is poor.He is happy.(yet)
10.I do not borrow money. I do not lend money.(neither …nor)
11.I trust her.She is honest.(because)
12.He did not come.He didn't inform me.(nor)
13.Anil passed the test.Surabhi also passed the test.(as well as)
14.He is very weak. He cannot walk.(too…to)
15.She is poor. She was proud.(Although)

Answers:

1. She is slow but sure.
2. Raju failed twice yet he would not stop.
3. Seema worked hard and secured first position.
4. She both cried and wept.
5. They were both punished and fined.
6. Neither play carom nor ludo.
7. Mend your ways or you will suffer.
8. He not only gave him shelter but also shared his secrets with him.
9. He is poor yet happy.
10.I neither borrow nor lend money.
11. I trust her because she is honest.

12. He did not come not did he inform me.
13. Anil as well as Surabhi passed the test.
14. He is too weak to walk.
15. Although she is poor she was proud.

13. Subject verb agreement

When a subject is with its correct verb, we called this *subject-verb agreement*.

In order to understand the rules of subject verb agreement we have to understand first the basic thing about making a noun and a verb plural.

To make a <u>noun</u> plural, we add **–s**

- Singular: Girl
- Plural: Girl<u>s</u>

To make a verb plural, we **take away** the **–s**.

- Singular: He talk<u>s</u>
- Plural: They talk.

Basic Rule: A singular subject takes a singular verb whereas a plural subject takes a plural verb.

Verbs in the present tense for third-person, singular subject (he, she, it and any other name/thing) have s-endings. Other verbs do not add s-endings.

singular	plural
I walk.	We walk.
You walk.	You walk.
He/ She /It walks.	They walk.
A boy walks.	Boys walk.
Teena walks.	Raj and Teena walk.

All kinds of verbs like '**do**', '**have**' **and** '**be**' follow this rule of subject verb agreement.

	SINGULAR	PLURAL
DO	He does.	They do.
HAVE	She has.	They have.
BE	He is.	We are.

The various rules of subject –verb agreement are given below one by one:

1. If there are two or more subjects joined by *and,* the subject must be plural, so the verb will also be plural.

Example-   Raj and William dance on the stage.

Exceptions-

- Breaking and entering is against the law.

- The bed and breakfast was charming.

In those sentences, *breaking and entering* and *bed and breakfast* are compound nouns.

2. If there are two or more subjects joined by *or,* the verb agrees with the part of the subject closest to it.

> The teacher or <u>the students</u> enter the classroom.
> The ministers or <u>the President</u> enters the room.
> Are either <u>my friends</u> or my uncle responsible?
> Is either <u>my sister</u> or my nephews responsible?

3. The indefinite pronouns *anyone, everyone, someone, no one, nobody* are always singular and, therefore, require singular verbs.

> Everybody **loves** grammar.
> Everyone **has** done his or her assignment.
> Somebody **has left** her pen.
> No one **cares** for time.
> Someone **knocks** the door.
> Nobody **was** there.

Some indefinite pronouns — such as *all, some* — are singular or plural depending on what they're referring to. If they refer to countable noun they will have plural verb .If they refer to uncountable noun they will have singular verb.

> Some of the <u>sugar</u> **is** wasted.
> Some <u>boys</u> **are** waiting.

On the other hand, there is one indefinite pronoun, *none*, that can be either singular or plural; it often doesn't matter whether you use a singular or a plural verb — unless something else in the sentence determines its number.

> None of the boys **have done** their homework.
> None of the bread **is** fresh.

4. Indefinite pronouns **'Everyone'** and **'Everybody'** are singular, so they must be followed by a singular verb. **Each** is often followed by a prepositional phrase ending in a plural word (Each of the boys).It may appear plural but it is always singular and requires a singular verb.

> Everyone has got a seat.
> Everybody has completed the form.
> Each of the students has completed the assignment.

5. The pronouns neither and either are singular and need singular verbs.

> Neither of the two girls was ready.
> Either of these watches is good.

6. Phrases such as *together with, as well as*, and *along with* are not the same as *and*. The noun that comes before these words will decide the nature of the verb.

> The manager as well as his brothers **is** going to prison.
> The shopkeepers as well as their leader **sit** in protest.
> The cap together with the shirts **is** cheap.
> Ram along with his team members **is** going to London.

7. 'There' and 'here' are never subjects. In sentences that begin with these words, the subject is usually found later on in the sentence.

> There were five books on the shelf. ('were' agrees with the subject 'books'.)
> Here is the report you wanted. ('is' agrees with subject 'report')
> There is no excuse for this lapse. ('is' agrees with the subject 'excuse')
> Here are some mangoes. ('are' agrees with the subject 'mangoes')

8. Sometimes modifiers will be found between a subject and its verb, but these modifiers must not confuse the agreement between the subject and its verb.

The minister, who has been jailed along with his four associates on charges of various frauds but who also seems, like a cat, to have several political lives, **is** finally going to jail.

9. Some nouns, while plural in form, are actually singular in meaning.

- Economics is (not are) an easy subject for some people.
- Aesthetics is (not are) taught by Prof. Paul.
- Mathematics is considered difficult by many students.

Some other such nouns are as given below-

Mumps	physics	social studies	economics
Measles	calisthenics	statistics	civics
Physics	gymnastics	phonics	news
Acrobatics	aesthetics	thesis	mathematics

10. Expressions of time, money, measurement, and weight are usually singular when the amount is considered one unit.

Fifty pounds is (not are) too much to ask.

Twelve days is (not are) not nearly enough time.

On occasion, however these terms are used in the plural sense.

There were thirty minutes to countdown.

11 Collective nouns may be singular or plural, depending on their use in the sentence.

A collective noun is a noun used to name a whole group. Following are some common examples:

army	bunch	orchestra
audience	flock	public

class	group	swarm
club	herd	team
committee	jury	troop
United States	crowd	battalion

The team is playing a very well. (Team is considered as one unit—singular.)

The Team were asked to give their educational backgrounds. (Team is considered as separate Individuals—plural.)

12. Fractional expressions such as one third of, half of, a percentage of, a majority of are sometimes singular and sometimes plural, depending on the meaning.

Some of the players are still angry.
A large percentage of the public is voting against him.
Two third of the troops were lost in the battle.
Forty percent of the workers body is in favor of changing the policy.
Two thirds of the garden was destroyed by fire.

13. Use a singular verb with distances, periods of time, sums of money, etc., when considered as a unit.

Five miles is too far to walk.
Seven years is the maximum sentence for that offence.
Ten pounds is a high price to pay.

14. The word '*were*' replaces '*was*' in sentences that express a wish or are contrary to fact:

If Dileep **were** here, you'd be sorry.
I wish it **were** Sunday.

15. Introductory 'it' is always singular.

It is my brother who comes here each day.
It is your rats which cause the trouble.

16. Some nouns are always plural and always take a plural verb-

Trousers   shorts   briefs   jeans

Pants   sunglasses   scissors   pliers   tweezers

- My trousers are old.
- Nowadays shorts are popular.
- Where are your scissors?

17. Generic reference takes plural verb. When any adjective with 'the' before it denotes a class a group of people etc. it takes plural verb.

The rich are happy.
The old hate loud music.
The young like to wear fashionable clothes.
The Americans are crazy for comfort and the Germans prefer technology.

Practice 1

Fill suitable verb to make meaningful sentences:

1. There ....a bus at 10a.m.[is/are]
2. Most of the boys...............gone home.[has/have]
3. What ....the latest news?[is/are]
4. A number of boys..............there.[is/are]
5. Each child............ice-cream.[has/have]
6. Cows ....us milk.[give/gives]
7. Does the boy...................English?[speak/speaks]
8. One of my friends ....a car.[has/have]
9. Mr. and Mrs. Collins ....in the garden.[is/are]
10. The Ganges ....a holy river.[is/are]

Answers (Practice 1)
1. There is a bus at 10 a.m.
2. Most of the boys have gone home.

3. What <u>is</u> the latest news?

4. A number of boys <u>are</u> there.

5. Each child <u>has</u> ice-cream.

6. Cows <u>give</u> us milk.

7. Does the boy <u>speak</u> English?

8. One of my friends <u>has</u> a car.

9. Mr. and Mrs. Collins <u>are</u> in the garden.

10. The Ganges <u>is</u> a holy river.

Practice 2

1. The people of the village.......hard working.[is/are]

2. More than sixty boys......passed in the exam.[has/have]

3. One of Mr. Paul's sons.............a doctor. [is/are]

4. Houses of this type......three rooms.[has/have]

5. The villages of our country ....poor.[is/are]

6. Neither he nor his wife......arrived.[has/have]

7. Most of the money ....lost.[is/are]

8. Neither of the boys ....able to win the race.[was/were]

9. A lot of food......lying there.[was/were]

10. Either Rana or Raju ....done this mischief.[has/have]

Answer (Practice 2)

1. The people of the village **are** hard working.

2. More than sixty boys **have** passed in the exam.

3. One of Mr. Paul's sons **is** a doctor.

4. Houses of this type **have** three rooms.

5. The villages of our country **are** poor.

6. Neither he nor his wife **has** arrived.

7. Most of the money **is** lost.

8. Neither of the boys **was** able to win the race.

9. A lot of food **was** lying there.

10. Either Rana or Raju **has** done this mischief.

Practice 3

1. Half of the apples................bad.[is/are]

2 More girls than one................invited.[was/were]

3 I wish I ....king. [was/ were]

4 Each man................a vote.[has/have]

5 The pen that you gave me ......lost.[is/are]

6 Nobody.............present.[was/were]

7. Mathematics ....a very interesting subject. [are/is]

8 The United States ....a big country. [is/are]

9 Gulliver's Travels...........a famous book. [is/are]

10. A large number of people ....applied for the job. [has/have]

Answer-(Practice 3)

1. Half of the apples are bad.

2 More girls than one were invited.

3 I wish I were a king.

4 Each man has a vote.

5 The pen that you gave me is lost.

6 Nobody was present.

7 Mathematics is a very interesting subject.

8 The United States is a big country.

 9 Gulliver's Travels is a famous book.

10. A large number of people have applied for the job.

Practice 4

 Choose the correct option given in the bracket to fill suitable verb in the blank in each sentence-

1. Your friend ....too much.(talk/talks)

2. The girls on the stage ....well.(dance/dances)

3. He ....dinner for his children.(cook/cooks)

4. The students...............to school every day.(go/goes)

5. The ground of the cricket matches........the ball.(bounce/bounces)

6. Some members of the team.............present.(is/are)

7. All of the milk.......................gone.(is/are)

8. Neither of the players ....here .(is/are)
9. Each of the teachers...................all the rules.(observe/observes)
10. Most of the tickets................ sold. (Was/were)

Answer (Practice 4): talks, dance, cooks, go, bounces, are, is, is, observes, were

Practice 5
Rearrange the following words to make meaningful sentences-
(i) wins/ the /slow/ steady/and /race
(ii) for/much/ not/this/nine/ rupees/ hundred/is/table
(iii) knows/no/one/ this /besides/secret/nurse/the
(iv) class /six/room/are /there/boys /in/the
(v) either/companions /or/his/he/guilty/were
(vi) to her/well known/are /you
(vii) I/you/am/in/as well as/ the /wrong
(viii) false /is /news/this
(ix) other/any/metal/than /iron/ useful/more/is
(x) teeth/morning /my/brush/I /every

ANSWERS:
(i) Slow and steady wins the race.
(ii)Nine hundred rupees is not much for this table.
(iii) No one besides this nurse knows the secret.
(iv) There are six boys in the classroom.
(v) Either he or his companions were guilty.
(vi) You are well known to her.
(vii) You as well as I am in the wrong.
(viii) This news is false.
(ix) Iron is more useful than any other metal.
(x) I brush my teeth every morning.

14. Verb Patterns

Pattern 1 : Subject +verb+ complement

    He is a doctor.

    This room is hot.

    Their car is imported.

Pattern 2: subject +Verb with object+ object

    They want you to help.

    He wants him to go.

    The people want the President to interfere.

    The public wants the king to act.

Pattern 3: Subject + verb+ one object

    They need some money.

    I want a pen.

    The nation requires a leader.

    The cow eats grass.

Pattern 4: Subject +verb +object+ object

    They offered her a job.

I gave him some books.

The students gave their teacher a gift.

The police asked the thief a question.

Pattern 5: Subject +verb +object+ object complement

They found the movie interesting.

I got the work completed.

The government declared the bill abandoned.

We saw the train leaving the station.

Pattern 6: Subject + verb (without object or complement)

The window opened.

The school closed.

The voters arrived.

The train disappeared.

The stars appear.

Pattern 7: Subject+ verb+ preposition +prepositional object

I am thinking about Joe.

He admired of her smartness.

These girls failed in their entrance test.

Pattern 8: Subject+ verb+ to infinitive

I want to leave.

They forgot to bring the tickets.

She decided to perform.

You preferred to stay there.

Pattern 9: Subject + verb+ noun/pronoun+ to infinitive

She requested him to stay.

I appealed him to interfere.

You advised me to appear in the test.

Who suggested you to wear this dress?

Pattern 10: Subject +verb+ gerund

I love dancing.

He prefers walking.

Mr. Pal enjoys swimming.

I dislike watching that film.

Pattern 11: Subject+verb+noun/ pronoun+ adjective

He turned the light off.

I prefer my tea hot.

The student left the door open.

I found the room wet.

Pattern 12: Subject +verb+ noun/pronoun+ present participle

I found him washing the car.

We noticed the leaves drying.

The police caught them playing cards.

The teacher saw us sitting on the floor.

She kept the milk boiling.

Pattern 13: subject+ verb+ noun/pronoun+ past participle

I saw the door opened.

You will get the clothes stitched.

He found the milk boiled.

They want the letters posted.

She found the address changed.

I had my shirt ironed.

Pattern 14: Subject+ verb+ noun/pronoun+ (to be) complement

I consider him lazy.

You will call him coward.

He considered me unfit.

They announced the team selected.

The Manager declared him honest.

The team members chose him captain.

Pattern 15: Subject+ verb+ that clause (object of the verb)

He believes that it will not rain today.

I think the train will reach in time.

The manager declared that the bonus will be doubled.

She hoped that she would get admission in that college.

He accepted that he copied the answers.

They reported that the food was stale.

Pattern 16: Subject+ verb+ interrogative +clause

I asked what he was doing.

He inquired where he got that watch.

They asked what I wished to do.

She did not know how to reach her home.

Some people knew how the fire broke out.

Pattern 17: Subject + verb + interrogative + to-infinitive etc.

He did not know how to get the reservation.

We did not know how to get a passport.

She did not remember how she reached there.

I know how to operate that phone.

John did not know what to do to get a job.

They will tell when to apply for the post.

Try to finalize where to go in the weekend.

Pattern 18: Subject + verb+ noun/pronoun+ interrogative +to infinitive.

They will tell you when to apply for a job.

I shall explain you how to get a passport.

He asked me where to get tickets.

He displayed us how to operate a computer.

She told us what to do next.

15. How: Manner, Means and Instrument.

How may be used to ask about manner, means or instrument for any action.

- In order to show the manner we use an adverb,
- to tell about means we use 'by+ means' and
- to tell about an instrument we use' with+ instrument'.

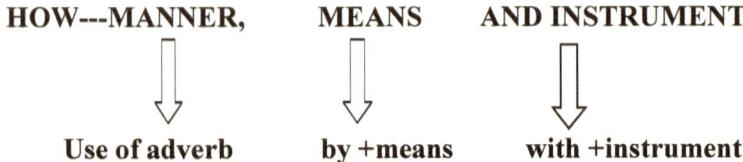

HOW---MANNER,   MEANS   AND INSTRUMENT

Use of adverb   by +means   with +instrument

Manner-
How did Radha dance?
Radha danced gracefully. (Manner)

How did he run?	He ran very fast.
How did she walk?	She walked slowly.
How did they speak?	They spoke confidently.
How did you cross the road?	I crossed the road carefully.

Means –

How do they go to market?
They go to market by bus.(means)

How did you withdraw the money?   I withdrew the money by cheque.
How did he send the message?   He sent the message by SMS.
How did she reach Boston?   She reached Boston by Airplane.

Instrument-

How did he remove the screw?
He removed the screw with a screw driver.

How did you cut the cake?   I cut the cake with a knife.
How did you write on the board?   I wrote on the board with a chalk.
How do they attach the papers?   They attached the papers with a pin.

16. Idioms

Idiom is a group of words established by usage as having a meaning not predictable from those of the individual words.

In other words an idiom is a word or phrase which means something different from its literal meaning.

For example there is an idiom in English 'to have a lot on' .It means 'to be very busy, to have lots to do'. It is used in the sentence thus- "I am sorry, I can't come on Monday, I've got a lot on that day. What about Tuesday?" Another use of the same idiom may be-"Raj hasn't got a lot on at the moment. He is waiting for the new project to start."

The list of some commonly used idiom is given below-

1. A blessing in disguise- something good that isn't recognized at first.

2. Add insult to injury-to worsen an unfavorable situation.

3. Action speaks louder than words-actions are more important than words

4. a piece of cake-easy

5. Ball is in your court-It is up to you to take the next step.

6. Best of both worlds- Having all the advantages/benefits.

7. Burn the midnight oil-to work late into the night.

8. Beating about the bush-not discussing what is important

9. Break a leg-wishing someone to do well

10. Can't stand something-to dislike something

11. Can't judge a book by its cover-cannot judge anything primarily on appearance

12. Easier said than done-easy to say but hard to actually do

13. Hang on a second-wait for a moment

14. Hang out-spend time with a friend

15. Hold your horses-wait/calm down

16. Make a key decision-make a crucial decision

17. Jump on the bandwagon-join a popular trend or activity

18. Keep something at bay- keep something away

19. Kill two birds with one stone-to accomplish two different things at the same time

20. Last straw-the final problem in the series of problems

21. Let the cat out of the bag-to share information that was previously concealed

22. Making long story short-come to the point-leave out details

23. On the same page- Having similar thoughts.

17. Phrasal Verb

In modern English it is very useful to place prepositions or adverbs after certain verbs so as to obtain a variety of meanings. We call them phrasal verbs. These phrasal verbs are very common in English. They are used very frequently. Here are two lists: one consists of some common verbs and the other consists of prepositions. Let's try to form phrasal verbs from them.

List A	List B
go	out
make	up
take	in
break	off
give	away

By combining them we can make a lot of new words such as:

make up	break off	give up	make out
break out	go away	take off	break in
go off	take out	break up	go out
take up	give away	go up	take in
give in	give out		

These are phrasal verbs. A phrasal verb consists of a verb and a preposition or adverb that modifies or changes the meaning.

'Give up' is a phrasal verb that means 'stop doing something' which is very different from 'give'.

The word or words that modify a verb in this manner can also go under the name particle. [**Particle**- An adverb or a preposition that can combine with a verb to make a phrasal verb is called a particle. In the phrasal verb 'give up', the word 'up' is a particle.]

The meanings and uses of some of the phrasal verbs are given below-

Ask for:

Meaning- 1.ask to, speak to:

- Go there and ask for the receptionist.She will give you all the information.

    2. Request, demand:

- The opposition **asked for** the minister's resignation.
- He **asked for** five days leave.

Be against (be opposed to) I am against going for a poll.

Be for (be in favor) We are all for going to Agra for a picnic.

Break out (begin, especially war/epidemic/fire etc.)-War broke out between two countries. Fire broke out because of short circuit.

Bring up (educate and train children) - He was brought up by his grandfather after his father's death.

Call off (cancel something not started yet ,or abandon something already in progress)- The management accepted the demands so the strike was called off by the union leader.

Carry out (perform duties/obey orders etc.)-Employees are to carry out their manager's order.

Do without (manage in the absence of a person or a thing).You cannot do without a mobile phone in the travel.

Get back (reach home again)-The children got back late after the party last night.

Give up (abandon an attempt)-The fox tried to reach the grapes but gave up after a few attempts.

Go through (examine carefully)-Go through this file and find out the proper steps.

Hold up (stop by threat or violence) –The robbers help up the bus and looted the travelers.

Keep on (to continue)- Keep on until you get to the post office.

Look for (search for, seek) – I am looking for my lost pen.

Make out(discover the meaning of, understand, see, hear etc.)-I cannot make out what you are saying.

Put down(crush rebellion ,movements)- The troops were used to put down the rebellion.

Wear out (exhaust)-I have travelled on foot all night. Now I am completely worn out.

Some more phrasal verbs are given below in the table-

Phrasal Verb	Meaning	Use
Abide by	accept/follow	You have to abide by what the court decides.
Account for	to explain	They had to account for all the losses of the company.
ask around	asking the same question to many	I have no idea but I will ask around to get the facts.
back up	support	You don't worry. I shall back you up.
Back out	withdraw	The army told the terrorists to back out.

Bear out	confirm	The research bears out the government's claim.
bear with	endure/ tolerate	Please bear with me a moment while I check the file
call up	phone	You should call up your brother now

call off	cancel	The manager called the meeting off.
call on	to pay a short visit to a person	I called on him last year when I went to Mumbai
come apart	separate	The tin roof came apart in the storm
come forward	volunteer	The student came forward with his assignment.
come across	to meet by chance/Discover	I came across this diary when I was cleaning the store
Drop in	visit without appointment	He may drop in anytime.
Drop out	discontinue	Raj dropped out of school due to shortage of money
Fall apart	break into pieces	The contents of the box fell apart.
fall off	decrease	The viewership of the channel fell off after that serial.
fend off	resist something successfully	He managed to fend off the controversy in the media.
find out	discover	Without an address it is difficult to find out anyone in this city.
fool around	not be serious	The teacher was angry as the

		students were fooling around.
Get away	escape	The thieves got away in the bicycle leaving everything.
Get on	become old	He is getting on now still he walks a lot.
Get over	overcome, recover	I just got over the fever and now my brother has it.
Give up	surrender, stop trying	Keep trying; never give up till you get success.
grow up	become an adult	He grew up in Australia.
Hang in	stay positive	Hang in there. I am sure you will get success soon.
hang out	spend time relaxing	They hang out at my room in place of going to the movie.
hold on	wait for a short time	Could you hold on for a minute? I am transferring your file.

keep up	continue at the same rate	If you keep up this progress you will get well soon.
let down	disappoint	I trust you fully .I hope you will not let me down
look after	take care of	I have to look after my ailing

		father.
look forward to	Be excited about	I am looking forward to the Autumn vacations.
make up	forgive each other	They quarreled at night, but they made up at breakfast.
pass away	die	Mr. Das passed away last night after a long illness.
put up with	tolerate	I can't put up with the loud noise of my neighbor's TV
run into	meet unexpectedly	I ran into Harriet last Friday at the post office.
run away	leave unexpectedly	The old man ran away from home and is missing now.
shop around	compare prices	You should shop around a little before selecting this shirt.

show off	act specially to invite attention	The children were showing off in the shopping mall.
stick to	continue doing/pursuing	The Government decided to stick to the new plan.
Turn off	switch off	You should turn off TV and fan

		before leaving the room.
Turn up	appear suddenly	Our boss turned up suddenly after a long leave.
Try on	sample clothing	You should try this shirt on before buying it.
Warm up	prepare for exercise	I always warm up by walking before running.
Wear off	Fade away	The flowers fade up in the heat of the afternoon.
Work out	exercise	I work out at the gym to keep fit.
Work out	be successful	Our plan worked out fine

Practice 1:Fill in the blanks with suitable phrasal verbs-

1. Quick! ....the bus. It's ready to leave.
2. I don't know where my book is. I have to ....it.
3. Its dark inside .Can you ....the light please?
4. ....the form please.
5. I need some new clothes. ''Why don't you ....these jeans?"
6. It's warm inside.   ....your coat.
7. This pencil is really old. You can ....
8. It's so loud here. Can you ....the radio a little.
9. The firemen were able to ....the fire in Church Street.
10. Does your little brother ....ghost?

Answers-

1. get on 2. look for 3. switch on 4 .fill in 5. try on 6. take off
7. throw it away 8.turn down 9. put out 10. believe in

Practice 2: Fill in the blanks with appropriate prepositions/adverbial particles:

(i) My servant asked ……three days leave. (after/for/out/to)
(ii)Fire broke……….in the post office last night.(in/into/out/off)
(iii)When our demands were accepted we called ……….the strike. (in/out/for/off)
(iv) I'll be in the office all day. I'll get ……late in the night. (back /out/in/on)
(v)The troops were called out to put…..rebellion. (up/on/down/off)
Answers :(i) for (ii)out   (iii)off   (iv) back (v)down

Practice3: Match the following phrasal verbs with their meaning –

Put out	collide
Run into	assume responsibility
Set out	exhaust
Take over	extinguish
Wear out	start a journey

Answer: put out- extinguish, run into- collide, set out- start a journey, take over- assume responsibility- wear out- exhaust.

Practice 4: Fill in the blanks with appropriate prepositions or adverbs-

(i) He kept ……….working till mid night (by/on/up)
(ii) He spoke in such a hurry, that I could not make……..what he said.(up/off/out)
(iii)I was looking …..my lost pen when my daughter told me it was on the table.(for/ out/about)
(iv)There are some mistakes in this draft. Go………it and correct them.(on/for/through)

(v)Our bus was held………..by some militants.(on/up/off)

(vi)You should carry………my orders, else you may lose your job. (on/for/out)

(vii) He brought ………the question of raising the salary of the staff in the meeting.(out/up/on)

(viii) It is very hot .I cannot do …………..a fan.(with/without/from)

(ix) The girl gave ………..his studies to take up a job (up/in/out)

(x) This work wears me …………completely. (On/ up/out)

Answers : (i)on (ii)out (iii)for   (iv) through (v)up (vi)out   (vii) up (viii)without   (ix)up   (x) out

18. Synonym and Antonym

Synonym-A word or phrase that means exactly or nearly the same as another word or phrase in the same language is called synonym of that word or phrase.

Antonym- A word that has the exact opposite meaning of another word is its antonym.

List of synonyms and antonyms

No.	Word	Synonyms	Antonyms
1.	abaft	astern, behind	front, ahead, leading
2	abandon	leave, abdicate ,desert, forsake	pursuit, quest, keep
3.	abase	confound, debase, mock, demean, shame	elevate, dignify, praise, exalt
4	Ability	Skill , aptitude	inability
5.	Abjure	renounce, recant	induct, welcome, accept
6	Able	Capable	unable

7	Above	Overhead	below
8	Abundant	plentiful	insufficient
9	Abuse	defame, vilify	respect, esteem
10	Accurate	Correct ,right	inaccurate

11	adapt	modify, adjust	
12	Achieve	attain, accomplish	Fail
13	Active	Energetic ,lively	inactive
14	Adamant	Firm, determined	Maneuverable
15	Add	Increase	Subtract,
16	Adequate	Sufficient, ample	insufficient ,inadequate
17	Adjourn	Postpone	Recommence, continue
18	Adult	Grown up	Child
19	Advocate	Support, recommend	Oppose
20	After	Following ,next	Before
21	Afraid	Frightened, scared	Courageous ,brave
22	Aggressive	pushy	Passive ,peaceful
23	Aid	Help ,assist	Hinder
24	Always	Forever	Never
25	Amateur	Beginner ,novice	Professional
26	Ambitious	Aspiring ,driven	unambitious
27	Antagonize	Provoke, embitter	Sooth, tranquilize
28	Apparent	Obvious ,seeming	Hidden, obscure
29	Approve	Accept, endorse	Disapprove
30	Arrive	Reach ,come	Depart, leave
31	Arrogant	Haughty	modest
32	artificial	Fake, synthetic	Real, authentic
33	Ask	Question ,inquire	Answer
34	Atrocious	Dreadful, contemptible ,vile	Kind, wonderful
35	Authentic	Genuine, real, factual	False, artificial
36	Average	Ordinary, fare	Unusual ,exceptional
37	Awful	Dreadful, atrocious	Pleasant
38	Awkward	Clumsy, uncoordinated	Graceful
39	Ban	Prohibit, forbid	Allow ,permit

40	Barren	Unproductive ,infertile	Fertile, productive
41	Bashful	Shy, timid	Outgoing ,assured
42	Beautiful	Pretty ,attractive ,lovely	Ugly
43	Before	Prior ,earlier	After, behind
44	Begin	Start ,initiate	Finish, end
45	Believe	Trust ,accept	Doubt, distrust
46	Below	Under ,lower	Above
47	Beneficial	Helpful ,useful, advantageous	Harmful ,adverse
48	best	Finest choice	Worst
49	Birth	Beginning	Death ,end
50	Blend	Combine , mix	Separate
51	Bottom	Base ,foundation	Top
52	Brave	Courageous ,heroic, bold	Cowardly ,timid
53	Break	Fracture ,burst	Repair ,heal
54	brief	Short ,concise	Long
55	bright	flashing, effulgent	dull, faded
56	broad	Wide ,expansive	Narrow
57	Busy	Active ,occupied, working	Idle, inactive
58	Buy	Purchase	Sell
59	Calm	Quiet, tranquil ,still	Excited, turbulent
60	Capture	Apprehend ,seize, arrest	Free, release
61	Caprice	whim, conceit	consistency, firmness
62	Care	Concern ,protection	Neglect
63	Careful	Cautious ,watchful	Careless ,reckless
64	Cease	Stop ,discontinue	Continue
65	Certain	Positive ,sure ,definite	Uncertain ,unsure
66	Charming	Delightful, appealing , enchanting	Obnoxious, gross , vulgar
67	Chilly	Cool ,nippy	Warm
68	Chubby	Plump , pudgy	Thin, skinny
69	Clarify	Explain , simplify	Confuse
70	Close	Shut , fasten	Open
71	Close	Near ,imminent	Far
72	Coarse	Bumpy ,rough	Fine smooth

73	Colossal	Enormous ,immense ,mammoth	Tiny, insignificant, trivial
74	Combine	Blend ,unite ,join	Separate
75	Comical	Amusing ,funny , humorous	Tragic, sorrowful
76	Complex	Complicated, intricate	Simple
77	Competent	Capable ,qualified	Incompetent , inept
78	Comprehend	Understand ,grasp	Confuse ,misinterpret
79	Complete	Conclude ,finish	Incomplete
80	Compress	Crush ,condense ,squeeze	Expand
81	Concrete	Real ,tangible ,solid	Abstract ,flimsy
82	Concur	Agree ,cooperate	Disagree
83	Condemn	Censure ,denounce	Approve
84	Condense	Compress ,concentrate	Expand ,enlarge
85	Confess	Admit ,acknowledge	Deny
86	Confine	Contain, enclose ,restrain	Free ,release
87	Conflict	Oppose ,differ ,clash	Agree
88	Conflict	Fight ,battle ,struggle	Peace ,harmony
89	Conform	Comply ,submit	Dissent ,dispute
90	Confuse	Complicate ,muddle ,jumble	Clarify
91	Congested	Overcrowded ,stuffed	Empty ,unfilled
92	Connect	Join ,link ,attach	Separate, disconnect
93	Conscientious	Scrupulous ,virtuous	Neglectful ,careless
94	Conscious	Aware ,cognizant	Unaware, unconscious
95	Consecutive	Successive ,continuous	Interrupted

96	Conservative	Cautious ,restrained	Radical ,extreme
97	Considerate	Thoughtful ,sympathetic, mindful	Thoughtless ,selfish
98	Constantly	Always ,continually	Scarcely ,seldom
99	Contaminate	Pollute ,defile ,infect	Purify
100	Contented	Satisfied ,pleased	Dissatisfied ,unhappy

101	conquer	subdue, defeat	
102	Correct	Accurate ,right , proper	Wrong ,incorrect
103	Courage	Bravery ,valor	Cowardice
104	Courteous	Polite ,civil	Rude
105	Cover	Conceal ,hide	Expose
106	Cranky	Cross, irritable	Good humored
107	Crazy	Insane ,daft ,mad	sane
108	Cruel	Mean ,heartless, ruthless	Kind ,humane
109	Cry	Sob ,weep	Laugh
110	dally	Loiter ,linger	Rush
111	damage	Hurt ,impair ,harm	Remedy ,repair
112	dangerous	Unsafe, hazardous , perilous	Safe
113	Daring	Bold ,audacious	Cautious
114	Dark	Dismal ,black	Light
115	Dawn	Daybreak ,sunrise	Evening
116	Dead	Lifeless, deceased	Alive ,active
117	Decay	Rot ,spoil	Bloom ,flourish
118	Deduct	Subtract ,remove	Add
119	Defend	Protect ,shield	Attack ,assault
120	Defy	Resist , challenge	Obey ,comply
121	Delicate	Fragile ,dainty	Sturdy
122	Demolish	Destroy , wreck	Restore
123	Denounce	Blame ,censure ,indict	Commend
124	Dense	Thick ,heavy , compressed	Sparse ,empty
125	Depart	Leave ,exit	Arrive
126	Deposit	Store ,place	Withdraw
127	deprive	strip,debar	give, add
128	Desolate	Barren ,forsaken	Dense, verdant
129	Despise	Hate ,detest ,loathe	Love
130	destitute	Poor, penniless	Wealthy
131	Destroy	Ruin ,wreck ,devastate	Restore
132	Eccentric	peculiar, unusual	normal
133	Empty	drain, upload	fill
134	encourage	promote, support ,urge	discourage
135	enemy	opponent ,foe	ally, friend

136	evil	bad, wrong, wicked	good
137	extravagant	extreme, excessive, luxurious	meager
138	fast	rapid, quick, swift	slow
139	fabulous	marvelous, amazing	unexciting
140	frank	candid, straightforward, blunt	evasive
141	fraud	cheat, deception	fairness, integrity
142	fresh	unused, new	old, stale
143	flaw	defect, fault, blemish	perfection
144	gallant	chivalrous, stately	ungentlemanly
145	gigantic	immense ,colossal, enormous	tiny, minute
146	give	present	take
147	good	nice ,fine, well-behaved	bad, awful
148	gorgeous	ravishing, dazzling, stunning	hideous, unattractive
149	govern	administer, command	obey, yield
150	help	aid, assist	hinder ,thwart
151	hold	grasp, grip, retain	release ,discharge
152	honest	truthful, sincere, frank	untruthful, insincere
153	huge	vast	small
154	humane	compassionate, forbearing, kind	cruel , inhumane
155	humble	modest	showy ,vain
156	idle	inactive	busy
157	ignorant	uninformed	knowledgeable
158	impartial	neutral, unbiased	prejudiced, biased
159	impatient	eager, anxious	patient
160	important	significant ,meaningful	unimportant ,meaningless
161	independent	self-reliant	dependent
162	insane	crazy ,mad	sane
163	intimacy	familiarity ,informality	haughtiness, distance
164	irrelevant	unrelated	relevant
165	join	connect	separate
166	jolly	cheerful ,merry	sad ,glum

167	joy	delight, pleasure	sadness
168	keep	save, protect	discard, lose
169	kind	tender ,benevolent	cruel ,inhuman
170	legible	readable	illegible
171	lure	attract	repel
172	migrate	immigrate	stationary
173	miser	spendthrift, cheapskate, scrooge, skinflint	
174	mysterious	secret, hidden, inexplicable	obvious, known, clear, plain
175	nice	pleasing ,fine	unpleasant
176	nervous	afraid, worried	confident
177	optimistic	confident, hopeful	pessimistic
178	ordinary	usual, average	unusual, remarkable
179	possible	feasible	impossible
180	postpone	adjourn ,delay	continue
181	pretty	lovely, beautiful	homely
182	quite	silent ,tranquil	noisy, rowdy
183	quit	abandon, cease, stop	continue ,remain, stay
184	radiant	luminous	dim
185	reliable	trustworthy	unreliable
186	safe	harmless, reliable	dangerous ,insecure
187	smooth	flat, even	rough
188	special	exceptional, particular	ordinary, usual
189	tall	high	short
190	torture	afflict ,oppress	comfort, support
191	trivial	insignificant ,worthless	important, crucial
192	urgent	crucial	trivial
193	virtuous	righteous ,irreproachable	sinful, wicked
194	vacant	unoccupied, empty	filled, occupied
195	vagabond	beggar, mendicant, tatterdemalion	
196	wealthy	affluent, opulent, well-to-do	destitute, needy, poor
197	wise	prudent ,sensible	dull, uneducated

198	yield	produce, provide	keep, retain
199	zeal	devotion, earnestness, excitement	apathy, indifference, detachment
200	zenith	peak, apex	bottom, base

19. Formation of some words

1. Formation of Nouns from verbs.

Verbs	Nouns
Accept	Acceptance
Advise	Advice
Approve	Approval
Attend	Attention
Admit	Admission
Bear	Bier
Bind	Bond
Bleed	Blood
Bless	Bliss
Break	Breach
Burn	Brand
Carry	Carriage
Choose	Choice
Collect	Collection
Donate	Donation
Decide	Decision

Deal	Dole
Deem	Doom, Ditch
Depend	Dependence
Dig	Dike
Drain	Drainage
Feed	Food
Flow	Flood
Float	Fleet
Gape	Gap
Grieve	Grief
Guide	Guidance
Govern	Governance
Injure	Injury
Liberate	Liberty
Live	Life
Lose	Loss
Marry	Marriage
Prove	Proof
Pass	Passage
Prosper	Prosperity
Remove	Removal
Rob	Robbery
Separate	Separation
Sin	Song
Sit	Seat
Speak	Speech
Strike	Stroke
Strive	Strife
Weave	Web

Formation of nouns form adjectives

Adjective	Noun
Dull	Dolt
Hot	heat
Proud	pride

Wide	width
Long	length
High	height
Child	childish
Brute	brutish
Able	ability
Active	activity
Anxious	anxiety
Attentive	attention
Attractive	attraction
Brave	bravery
Broad	breadth
Bright	brightness
Confident	confidence
Coward	cowardice
Cruel	cruelty
Deep	depth
Distant	distance
Easy	ease
Famous	fame
Fertile	fertility
Generous	generosity
High	height
Impressive	impression
Knowledgeable	knowledge
Laughable	laughter
Multiple	multiplications
Obedient	obedience
Original	originality
Personal	personality
Proud	pride
Quarrelsome	quarrel
Receptive	receiver
Religious	religion
Sad	sadness
Sharp	sharpness

Sufficient	sufficiency

Formation of Adjectives form verbs

Verbs	Adjectives
Act	active
Admire	admirable
Believe	believable
Depend	dependant
Float	Fleet
Forget	forgetful
Heal	healthy
Lie	low
Measure	measurable
Obey	obedient
Possess	possessive
Quarrel	quarrelsome
Regret	regretful
Save	safe
Suspect	suspicious

Formation of verbs from nouns

Nouns	Verbs
Bath	Bathe
Belief	Believe
Blood	Bleed

Breath	Breathe
Brood	Breed
Cloth	Clothe
Drop	Drip
Food	Feed
Glass	Glaze
Gold	Gild
Grass	Graze
Half	Halve
Knot	Knit
Price	Prize
Sale	Sell
Sooth	Soothe
Tale	tell
Thief	Thieve
Wreath	Wreathe

Formation of verbs from adjectives

Adjective	verb
awake	awaken
black	blacken
bright	brighten
broad	broaden
chaste	chasten
damp	dampen
dark	darken
fast	fasten
flat	flatten
glad	gladden
high	heighten
long	lengthen
loose	loosen
mad	madden
moist	moisten
quick	quicken
sharp	sharpen

soft	soften
straight	straighten
strong	strengthen
sweet	sweeten
thick	thicken
tough	toughen
weak	weaken
white	whiten
wide	widen